TI

MW01518049

the ABCs
of Law School

a practical guide to success
without sacrifice

Ramsey Ali

Daniel Batista

Koker Christensen

Ian Cooper

The ABCs of Law School
© Irwin Law Inc., 2002

All rights reserved. No part of this publication may be reproduced, stored in a retrieval system, or transmitted, in any form or by any means, without the prior written permission of the publisher or, in the case of photocopying or other reprographic copying, a licence from CANCOPY (Canadian Copyright Licensing Agency), One Yonge Street, Suite 1900, Toronto, Ontario, M5E 1E5.

National Library of Canada Cataloguing in Publication

The ABC's of law school : a practical guide to success without sacrifice / Ramsey Ali ... [et al.].

ISBN 1-55221-065-0

1. Law—Study and teaching—Canada. 2. Law schools—Canada. 3. Law students—Canada. I. Ali, Ramsey, 1970-

KE307.A23 2002 340′.071′171 C2002-903688-7

Published in 2002 by
Irwin Law
One First Canadian Place
Suite 930 - Box 235
Toronto, ON
M5X 1C8

The Publisher acknowledges the financial support of the Government of Canada through the Book Publishing Industry Development Program (BPIDP) for our publishing activities.

Book design by George Kirkpatrick
Printed and bound in Canada,

1 2 3 4 5   06 05 04 03 02

For Manny

Summary Table of Contents

Detailed Table of Contents

Introduction

Two types of people read introductions: those flipping through a book in order to gauge its usefulness before buying it, and those who have already bought the book and want to get a sense of its overall direction before delving into the substantive material in the numbered chapters. This introduction will address the concerns of both types of reader.

If you are of the first type, one simple question is of primary concern to you: "Why *this* book?" That question seems all the more pertinent given that there is a wealth of material out there on the subject of law school. What separates this book from all those others? The answer to that question lies, most obviously, in this book's focus. Unlike previous books on the subject, which deal with a wide array of topics ranging from how to get into law school to which extra-curricular activities to pursue, this book focuses on a very narrow topic, but one which is of paramount importance to most law students: how to achieve academic success in law school without giving over one's entire life to the study of law.

Notice the qualifier we added in the last part of the foregoing sentence. We take it for granted that anyone who has read even this far probably has a keen interest in getting good grades. But we also understand that there is something else most law students are keenly interested in: having a life! Any advice we give in this book is respectful of that fact. For, even accepting that there may be many ways to skin the proverbial cat, we believe that (other things being equal) those that are most enjoyable and least taxing are to be preferred. You might therefore think of this book as a guide to achieving academic gain without suffering social—and hence psychological—pain. Indeed, this is a second, and perhaps more important, respect in which our book distinguishes itself from similar books.

Sound too good to be true? It isn't. The key to understanding how all this is possible lies in realizing that there is a great deal of myth surrounding the kernel of truth in what you may have already heard and read about law school. Part of our task as authors will be to strip away the layers of myth so that the reader can get at the vital core of useful information that lies beneath. In fact, we can begin at once with this process of debunking myth, and hence demystifying law school, by pointing out that the difficulty of law school is not all that it's cracked up to be. Although much of what you may have already heard rightly emphasizes the need for new law students to prepare themselves to face unfamiliar challenges, in our opinion the immensity of these challenges is usually overstated. It is undeniably true that prospective first-year law students must be ready to digest a lot of material (perhaps more than they are accustomed to), as well as prepare for and endure one hundred percent final exams. To make matters worse, a great deal—no less than one's future employment prospects—seems to ride on how well one meets these challenges. But this is no cause for alarm. As with all challenges, the secret to overcoming these ones lies in having a suitably systematic approach to dealing with them. That is what this book provides. This is the third way our book is different from other books on the same topic. Although other books provide some useful hints (not to mention some that are less than useful) for surviving law school, they almost never set out a suitably systematic approach to the problem of law school.

Of course this prompts the question: "What on earth is meant by the phrase 'a suitably systematic approach'?" Take first the word "systematic." A simple anecdote explains the term. A certain acquaintance of ours, having just received his first-year grades, remarked to one of us that being a top-notch law student had less to do with being "smarter" than one's peers than it had to do with "knowing how to work the system." He was quite bitter about what he perceived to be the grave injustice that his superior intellect had not been rewarded by the law school system. Whatever the impetus for his comments, however, we believe that he tripped over quite a valuable insight. Our only quibble with his lucid statement is that it tends to create a bit of a false disjuncture. While this person's own self-image could not allow him to see this at the time, our view of the matter (to paraphrase a well-known line from a recent movie) is that "smarter is as smarter does." The student who plays the system properly, and therefore achieves his or her academic goals with a minimum of effort, is a "smarter" student (whatever his or her IQ). Indeed, in our view, knowledge of how to work the system is the hallmark of the better—because smarter—law student.

It is important to realize, in connection with this last point, that what one needs in order to be a better law student is not knowledge of any old system, but knowledge of how to play "*the* system." It's because of this that we have emphasized the need for a *suitably* systematic approach. Not all systematic approaches to law school are created equal. Indeed, how could they be? It would be as much to suppose that just any old system for solving, say, a chess problem was as good as any other. But nobody would maintain with any degree of seriousness that a systematic analysis of every legal move on the board is a good way of solving a given chess problem, even if it does eventually lead to the correct solution. Chess problems, not unlike law school itself, confront us with a set of difficulties that have certain important and identifiable features and characteristics. These features and characteristics serve to guide and constrain the proper approach to the problem. A good chess book helps one acquire a feel for the salient features and characteristics of different positions on the chessboard, and hence develop a suitably systematic approach to any given problem. Likewise, we'll give the reader a sense of what constitutes the special problem posed by the law school experience so that he or she can better learn to play "*the* system."

None of this is to suggest, of course, that the reader must follow the advice set out in this book down to the last detail, nor that he or she must adopt our system with the religious fervour of a disciple who has heard the truth as if spoken from on high. We believe a strength of this book—and another way in which it differs from other books of its kind—is that it accommodates personal differences. We understand that students have a host of interests and goals, so our book is not aimed exclusively at producing straight A students. Indeed, that's precisely the point of offering a how-to guide directed at helping you achieve your academic goals *and* maintain a rich life outside of law school. Depending on how you prioritize these (sometimes) conflicting goals, you may choose to follow more or less of the advice contained in the pages that follow. But whatever your goals — even if you have only modest academic aspirations and wish to live an especially vibrant social life rather than be at the top of your class — you will find that the system contained in this book has plenty to offer. It sets out basic strategies and principles aimed at maximizing the results of your academic efforts (however great or small) by freeing time and mental energy for the pursuit of your other goals and interests. Again, this is not a book about defining those goals and interests. That task is left to you, the reader. What this book has to offer is a way to optimize the academic results that are such a central focus of most law students and their future employers without sacrificing other pursuits — be they social, intellectual, or charitable.

However, even the need to balance academic success with one's other interests imposes a kind of constraint on what qualifies as a suitable systematic approach to law school, confirming that not all systems are of equal worth. Law schools are full of students who fail to strike the right balance, either by focusing almost exclusively on academic success and letting their other interests fall by the wayside (a failing that much of the literature on law schools seems to encourage) or by letting their outside interests interfere too much with the pursuit of their academic goals. The problem with these students is not that they fail to be systematic in their pursuits. In a sense, they are all being a bit *too* systematic, for their respective systems leave little room for alternative, and equally important, pursuits. Consequently, those respective systems make equal, but opposite, mistakes. The system outlined in this book is intended to help you steer a safe course between the Charybdis of prioritizing academics to the exclusion of all else, and the Scylla of leaving no room for academic success in the pursuit of other interests. We will nevertheless spend a fair bit of time discussing these mistaken alternative systems, for we believe that it is only by being intimately familiar with the perils that threaten to waylay the prospective law student that she can set an appropriate course for herself.

Finally, since our mode of presentation is a further respect in which this book differs from others of its kind, a word or two should be said about how we propose to do all this. Instead of simply setting out the Dos and Don'ts of law school in the standard — and, in our view, rather dry — form, we present our system as an allegory of sorts. In other words, another difference between this book and others of its kind is that it instructs by example rather than by pre-scription. Accordingly, the systematic approach to law school that we advocate is embodied in a character named Andie. Of course, Andie is not the only protagonist in this story. As one might expect to find in any allegory worthy of the name, Andie has certain foils: in this case, Billie and Charlie. More will be said about each character later. For now, it suffices to indicate that Billie embodies the approach of those who pursue academic success to the exclusion of all else, whereas Charlie symbolizes those who let their academic perform-ance slip for the sake of other pursuits. By tracing the patterns of behaviour of each of our three main characters through the law school semester, up to and including preparation for and writing of the final exams, we expect to impart a great deal of practical wisdom concerning the law school system. The reader will learn as much about how to approach law school in a suitably systematic fashion from the foibles of Billie and Charlie as from Andie's successes.

There are, admittedly, more straightforward ways in which the material in this book could have been presented. Our justification for using these characters as allegorical vehicles for the carriage of valuable insights is quite simple. We aim to entertain as well as to inform. Our own experience, and no doubt yours as well, indicates that one learns best when one is interested and engaged (incidentally, this is an insight that forms an important part of Andie's winning law school strategy). To the extent that the chosen mode of presentation is more entertaining than standard modes — and we think you'll agree that it is — while at the same time remaining clear and accessi-ble, no further justification of it is therefore necessary.

Now, if all this hasn't already convinced you that this book offers a unique and useful approach to doing well in law school, there is one other thing we should mention. Unlike most books of its kind, our book has the advantage that the advice it gives is all based on recent first-hand experience: it is, in other words, a book that is written *by* students *for* students. Thus, the system set out in these pages is one that has been tested in a trial by fire, as it were. And in the end it has been judged successful by four students with goals and achievements as disparate as one might expect to find within a range of students who all care to varying degrees both about academics and about other interests quite apart from law school. If it worked for all of us, it can work for you too. It's now time to begin seeing how.

A General Outline

Our Three Stars

Meet Billie. Actually, if you've ever spent even a single day around law school, you've probably already seen him[1] around, most likely in the library. Since you will not have been able to put a name to him until now, however, consider this your first real introduction. All that you'll ever want to know (though certainly not all you'll *need* to know) about Billie can be conveyed by relating how we ourselves had the (mis)fortune of making Billie's acquaintance. As it happened, he made his own introduction before we ever stepped foot inside a law school. Billie was a prominent contributor to the orientation material we received the summer before our first year. Included in that material was a series of testimonials from students who had completed first year the previous spring. The one that made the greatest impression on us claimed that the effort involved in succeeding at law school exceeded anything that our previous experiences could possibly have prepared us for. Here's how Billie described it. Over the course of the semester, every case would need to be read, summarized, and reviewed numerous times. Every detail would need to be examined, re-examined, and absorbed. Intensive studying for exams, we were told, happened during the semester, not just during exam period. Therefore, it would be necessary not only to read the

---

1 We caution the reader against drawing conclusions about our use of gender pronouns throughout this book. We have adopted a convention of using the female pronoun in connection with Andie, and the male pronoun in connection with the other characters. In our view this was the easiest way to avoid confusion when discussing other characters in relation to Andie. Of course, all of our characters, including Andie, could just as easily be male or female.

assigned reading each week but also to summarize it and reread each and every summary we had made for every previous week. This was the picture of a successful law student. To cap things off, the sacrifice involved in becoming such a student could not be measured in terms of mere time alone. Billie claimed to have lost his perfect vision during first year, requiring glasses for the first time as a result of his diligent efforts.

Now meet Charlie. Again, you may have seen Charlie around the law school, but *certainly* not in the library (*quelle horreur!*) and probably only among the upper-year crowds. That's because Charlie is a bit of a latecomer to law school (and in more ways than one, as you'll eventually discover). If you're just beginning first year, you likely won't catch a glimpse of him among your fellow new initiates to the school, but he may join your class shortly after mid-year marks are released, and he'll certainly make his appearance by second year. Once he arrives, however, Charlie will quickly begin to make his (social) presence felt. Catch up with him in the student lounge — or, even better, in the local pub where you can share conversation over a pint or two — and Charlie will be only too eager to offer you his own theory on how to approach law school. That theory might best be captured in a slogan to the effect that "law school is a casino vacation." The two basic tenets underlying this theory are: first, that law school grades are really a matter of brute chance (a roll of the dice in an expensive casino, as it were); and second, that one should therefore spend less time studying and more time having fun, less time working and more time vacationing.

Now this, of course, is an odd-sounding theory for anyone to advance, let alone a law school student (we are, after all, generally recognized for our work ethic). Understanding its genesis, however, will help explain why Charlie takes his own sweet time in coming on the law school scene. The explanation goes something like this. Bewildered by his experiences in first year (or sometimes even in first semester), Charlie reflects back on the year and concludes that there is no rational connection between one's efforts during the year and the grades one receives at the end. It is not uncommon to hear him say, "I loved that class. I did every reading, went all the time, studied like mad and *still* got a C+. That other class? Hated it! Never went, barely read a thing and somehow got an A. It makes no sense." Understandably puzzled, Charlie concludes that the only solution is to approach law school in a somewhat more leisurely fashion, blowing off his studies and letting the chips fall where they may.

We would venture that Billie and Charlie are recognizable characters at just about every law school in North America. And their respective systems for law school "success" are the two dominant approaches to law school. It takes only a moment's reflection, however, to realize that both approaches leave something to be desired. If being like Billy — working oneself to death and ignoring the rest of one's life in the process — is the key to succeeding, then most of us are likely to conclude that success is not worth the sacrifice. On the other hand, if one's efforts do not change one's results, then one need not conclude along with Charlie that success is a matter of luck: it may well be that one's efforts are simply misdirected.

There is, of course, a better way. It is reflected in the approach to law school adopted by Andie, who takes it seriously and has found a way to remedy the deficiencies in the approaches of both Billie and Charlie. In fact, Andie's own systematic approach to law school is defined by reference and contradistinction to the strengths and weaknesses in the approaches of her two counterparts. Andie takes what is best in their approaches and makes it her own, discarding what is worst. Of course, this raises the question of how it is that Andie's approach for achieving a happy and successful law school career, which is what game theorists would call the "dominant strategy" (that is, best in all possible circumstances), has nevertheless been *statistically* dominated by these lesser strategies when it comes to actual practice of the law school "game." In order to address this question, and because Andie's approach takes its bearings from these failed approaches, let us spend a bit more time getting acquainted with Billie and Charlie.

A Tale of Three Characters (or The Evolution of the Law Student Species)

In the beginning, law school sets all of us up to be Billies. Even before we get there, we've all been told countless stories about how difficult law school is, how smart you have to be to do well, how hard you have to work. At first, most of us figure "No sweat. I'm a fairly smart person. I can work hard when I have to. Hell, isn't that how I got into law school in the first place?" But then we get there, and we're told that we'll be graded to a predetermined average mark. This is where things start to get ugly. What this means, of course, is that we're playing a "zero-sum game" with each and every one of our classmates. In other words, any gain made by one member of the class in terms of scoring above the average grade comes at the expense of one or more other members of the class, who must correspondingly be given something less than the average grade. If we all write great exams, we won't all get As: some of us will still get Cs and C+s. That's just what being graded on a curve implies. So it looks as though being "fairly smart" and working hard "when we have to" just isn't going to cut it anymore. Indeed, *all* of us are fairly smart and we *all* work hard when we have to: again, that's precisely how we got into law school. If we want to do well, then, it looks as though we're going to have to be *smarter* and/or work *harder* than our average classmate. And if we want to be on the Dean's List—which most of us do, since that's where we've always been before—we're going to have to be smarter and/or work harder than *90 percent* of our classmates!

For many of us, all this gives rise to the following chain of reasoning. "Look, I can't control how smart I am relative to other members of the class (though I'm certainly not prepared to concede anything). What I *can* control, however, is how hard I work. And I'm pretty certain that I can outwork most of these people if I put my mind to it. In fact, I'm prepared to prove it. That ought to *guarantee* me success! Oughtn't it?" Of course, since virtually every other member of the class is reasoning in the same fashion, the only thing guaranteed here is that the law school equivalent of an arms race is going to develop (the Hobbesians among us might choose to call it a war of each against all), with each student going to further and further lengths to outdistance the efforts of his classmates. And since every student is in more or less direct competition with every other student, "work" in this context means work *alone*. To be sure, students may join study groups—indeed, they may be *forced* to in order to keep pace with their peers—but their participation in such groups will inevitably be coloured by the fact that their fellow group members are, at the end of the day, their competitors. Thus study "group" is for them less a cohesive exercise in teamwork and more a grudging and unstable alliance struck with like-minded atomistic individuals whose pursuit of their own self-interest cannot help but interfere with the success of the group as a whole. For the most part, at any rate, studying is to be done not with a group, but in the solitude of a library cubicle with only one's books to keep one company and only the scratch of one's pen furiously taking notes to punctuate the lonely silence.

So it is that first-year law school gives birth to a preponderance of Billies. Needless to say, however, Billie's law school life is destined to be solitary, poor, nasty, brutish, and (with apologies to the purists among our Hobbesian friends) seemingly interminable. To add insult to injury, the desire for academic success that motivates Billie to adopt such a lifestyle is likely to go unfulfilled. It is after all highly doubtful that academic success can be attained by sheer dint of effort where one is in direct competition with others who are no less diligent.

These realizations are the seeds from which eventually there will spring to life a new breed of law school student: Charlie. While it is not entirely inconceivable that there will be a Charlie or two amidst the host of Billies scurrying around in the early days of first-year law, it is far more likely that Charlie will emerge only later, as a kind of "reformed" Billie (to hear Charlie himself tell it), one who has "seen the light" and "changed his losing ways." For there will be a subclass of Billies almost from the very start of the year, who are loathe to take part in what they rightly recognize as an arms race of sorts. Even if such a race was worth winning—and this is questionable, given the amount of effort involved—it is unclear to them what it would take to win it. There is, after all, only so much time in the day: surely, not *all* of it is to be spent working! Those who are already having these thoughts, though still firmly rooted in the Billie camp, are an incipient species of Charlie: Proto-Charlie, if you will. Unfortunately, at this early stage of his law school career, Proto-Charlie is not yet prepared to drop out of the race since he is still committed to being the successful student he has always been and sees no way to achieve that goal outside of being a reluctant participant.

It is only when Proto-Charlie ultimately does withdraw from the arms race that he will have shrugged off his allegiance—if not his ancestral ties—to the Billie camp and evolved into a full-blown species of Charlie. When he does so, alas, it will not be that he has had a great epiphany or finally summoned up the courage to do what every Billie would do had he but the sagacity and strength of will. No, Charlie's motivations are far less heroic than that, whatever he may tell you. Charlie drops out of the race because he sees himself losing and is afraid to confront what he thinks this must mean. You see, Charlie wholeheartedly buys into Billie's formula for academic success (not surprisingly, since he himself was once a Billie). For him, as for Billie, academic success is the product of: (1) one's own native intelligence, as measured in one's IQ score, for example; and (2) how hard one works, as measured, say, in a log recording the number of hours one devotes to studying.

Thus when Charlie begins to worry that he will not do as well — or actually *sees* himself not doing as well — as he might have wanted, he is faced with a crisis of confidence. He knows that he cannot attribute it to lack of effort, since up until now he has been grinding away with the best of the Billie bunch. That leaves only one other possibility, and there is *no way* Charlie is going to admit to himself, let alone to others, that his lack of success is due to a want of intelligence. So he simply drops out of the race; he stops working. Now he has a convenient rationalization for his lack of academic success (whether actual or anticipated): comparative lack of effort. Admittedly, holding oneself out as shiftless and uninterested may not appear to be an ego-enhancing move at first blush, but when compared with the horrible alternative — that most terrifying and unspeakable of all law school secrets ("I'm just not smart enough") — seeming lazy to others can start to look pretty good.

In any event, Charlie doesn't simply stop at portraying himself as lazy. In order to really sell the image he wants to project, and allow his ego to escape unscathed, Charlie presents his laziness as *justified* laziness. "Law school grades bear little or no relation to the amount of effort you put in, let alone the quality of your work," he tells us. "It's all about luck. The Prof takes his stack of exams and simply chucks them down a flight of stairs. Grades are then determined according to how far the exams happened to travel." (We're not putting words in Charlie's mouth, believe it or not. You're bound to come across this theory yourself once you've spent sufficient time around a law school, and it's not often clear whether those espousing it are being facetious.) "What point is there to working hard, in light of this? One may as well get on with the business of enjoying the rest of one's life and simply go through the necessary motions when it comes to school." Thus, in one fell swoop, Charlie manages not only to provide a justification for his laziness but also to generate a second rationalization for his disappointing grades: he's not just lazy; he's also unlucky.

As if this were not enough, Charlie then proceeds to add the finishing touches to his carefully crafted public image. Not only is his approach to law school justified in the sense of being rational, he suggests, but it is also justified in the sense of being spiritually enlightened. His whole demeanour implies that those who continue to toil away inside their little library cubicles are really just lost souls — they seek fulfillment in the chance and arbitrary recognition of an unfair grading system. Charlie, of course, fancies himself above such mundane pursuits. His attention is directed at matters of more lasting and universal importance: the social bonds that bring us together in community, for instance. Very soon Charlie's "spiritual enlightenment" begins to come off as holier than thou. Billie becomes an object of derision: he is at best to be pitied, and at worst to be scoffed at, for having damned himself to such a life of misery. Indeed, to hear Charlie tell it, he is the Buddha-like figure seeking enlightenment in the midst of uptight and all too competitive squares who spend their nights ripping out pages from library books and, when exam time comes, ripping out their hair as well.

By now, however, Charlie has begun to betray himself. For even if one could accept, against one's better judgment and only for the sake of argument, that the law school grading system is unfair, that its results are random, to now suppose that Charlie is past having any care for his academic performance strains credulity far beyond what one could reasonably be expected to tolerate. To begin with, he doth protest a bit too much. But more than that, he forgets who he is and where he came from. At the end of the day, Charlie, like the rest of us, is just another law student. He managed to secure that status precisely by displaying constant concern for the very thing for which he now disavows any care. If academic success and all its entailments are now to be considered matters of menial importance, Charlie owes us an explanation of why they ever mattered to him. Nay, he owes us an explanation of why he *continues* onward with the law school enterprise. Why not turn one's back on law school altogether and devote one's *entire* attention to more enlightened pursuits? Why even go through the motions? Finally, why, if grades are so insignificant, is the arbitrariness of the law school grading system "unfair"? In what sense is Charlie hard done by when the system fails to accord him the recognition that, by his own lights, does not matter to him?

These questions are, of course, all unanswerable. The proof of this is that, under pressure of exams, Charlie is invariably driven by guilt and fear to re-embrace those commitments that he once held but has since foresworn. Which only renders the questions all the more pressing. Indeed, their very importance provides the impetus for a new breed of law student to evolve: Andie. In Andie we find the culmination of the law school evolutionary process and, not surprisingly, its highest form of species. Like Charlie, Andie sees the failings in Billie's approach to academic success. She too is unwilling to enter into an arms race that can be won, if at all, only by giving one's entire life over to the study of law. For her, as for Charlie, this would involve committing herself to a life of torment, and with no clear compensation for her sacrifice. In fact, Andie recognizes in Charlie the refutation of Billie's approach to law school, the proof that hard work alone cannot guarantee academic success, that eventually one must either drop out of the race or face the probability that all one's efforts will have been for naught. If others continue to adhere to the Billie approach to law school even after it has failed to produce results, Andie understands that they are labouring under two mistaken beliefs. First, they think that they can objectify their worth as students, if not in their grades, then in the esteem and admiration their work ethic may elicit from others. Second, they fear that to drop out of the race at this point would be to lose their only chance even at mediocrity. They are right, Andie realizes, to attribute their mediocrity to the Billie approach, but not for the reasons they think. Being Billies is not their redemption; it is their damnation. It is not what prevents their slipping still further down the ranks of academic underachievers; it is what holds them down.

Still, while in Andie's view it would be preferable to submit to being beaten with a billy-club than to join the Billie club, she also realizes that Charlie is no angel. What Charlie tries to pass off as "spiritual enlightenment," Andie recognizes as a merely partial truth. Because it is only *partial*, Andie sees it as deficient, leaving something to be desired. No doubt there are other pursuits, quite apart from academic success, that are worthy and deserving of our attention: social interaction is perhaps chief among them. But it does not follow that academic success is rendered undesirable by that fact alone, nor that it should be eschewed as a base, mundane, or unworthy pursuit. If Billie is lost or misguided, it is not in his choice of ends but merely in the means he adopts in pursuit of those ends. Charlie's motivations for suggesting otherwise, Andie is well aware, lie partly in a desire to exalt his own laziness (in addition to merely justifying it) and partly in a desire to be able to proclaim publicly that he does not want what he privately fears he cannot have.

In the end, Charlie's private fear is as unfounded as Billie's parallel fear that it is only through incessant toil that he can continue to live up to his present standard of mediocrity. Both fears are based on the same misconception: the assumption shared by Billie and Charlie that academic success can be reduced to a straightforward formula combining standard intelligence and good old-fashioned hard work. It is by calling this assumption into question for the first time that Andie is able to overcome the deficiencies in the respective approaches to law school taken by her two counterparts. Andie realizes that this assumption has caused Billie to place an overemphasis on pure sweat of the brow, in the hope that he will thereby compensate for any deficiencies he may have in the area of raw intelligence. At the same time, it has caused Charlie to construct an alter-ego that devalues the importance of academic success in an effort to shield his actual ego from both: (1) the realization that, in his case, sweat of the brow has come up short of achieving that success; and (2) his fear that the blame for this shortcoming must lie in his own native ability. If only Billie and Charlie could come to see that it is not a lack of raw intelligence that impedes their progress, but a mistaken view of what academic success requires, they could begin to build on what is best about their respective theories. Thus Billie could come to see that Charlie is right to emphasize the importance of interests outside of law school and, conversely, Charlie could come to recognize that the importance of those other interests needn't take anything away from the equally important goal of doing well academically.

Of course, Andie is able to see all this and more. Freed of the false assumption that Billie and Charlie are in the grips of, Andie knows that if we *must* formulate academic success as a product of intelligence and work, then we're going to have to start defining our terms somewhat differently. No longer will it be appropriate to define "work" in terms of the brute number of hours dedicated to poring over law school materials. For this, of course, is precisely what originally led Billie down his socially ruinous path of conduct. Nor will it be acceptable to define intelligence according to some number that a standardized IQ test might spit out. The unexamined premise that such a number could ever be determinative of law school success is one that has always been of dubious quality and — as the tribulations of Billie and (especially) Charlie make clear — destructive influence. The only measure of intelligence that Andie recognizes as significant for the purposes of predicting academic success is one that relates directly to one's work habits. In other words, Andie knows that the key to success as a law student lies, not in being smarter and/or working harder than one's peers, but simply, and without qualification, in *working smarter.*

one

The BUILDING BLOCKS of LAW SCHOOL SUCCESS

THIS short history now complete, the following question arises: What exactly is intended by our invocation of a phrase as hackneyed as "work smarter"? To answer that question fully would require that we explain at this stage everything that it is the task of this entire book to explain. Nevertheless, we can begin by making some preliminary observations. Notice, for starters, that Andie's formula for law school success is not built around working smarter "than one's peers." To repeat, it is simply, and without qualification, built around working smarter. The temptation to calibrate one's efforts in response to what one's classmates are doing is exactly what must be avoided if one wants to steer clear of Billie's fate and avoid an arms race.

Rest assured, however, that in working smarter (full stop) Andie will also be working smarter than most of her peers. For, while Andie may be the most evolved of all law school species, she is far from having the most numerical representation at law school. (It is, in fact, part of the goal of this book to render other less developed species extinct; for now, however, these dinosaurs continue to dominate the law school landscape.) Thus, it will be all too easy for Andie to work smarter than Charlie, for example, since Charlie simply does not work. As for Billie, Andie is assured of outsmarting his work habits because she has developed her own work habits largely in response to the failings that she has observed in his. But while Andie goes out of her way to outsmart Billie's work habits, this should not be confused with trying to work smarter *than her peers*. There is no contradiction here: if all her peers were to shed their affiliation with the Billie camp and join the Andie camp tomorrow, her work habits would not change in response to this. Andie's interest is not in out-doing her peers *per se*, but in outsmarting the work habits of "Billie," conceived of as a general *type* of student, rather than as any particular individual.

Andie Is a SOCIAL SPECIES of Law Student

The distinction just made is important because it gives rise to an insight that is at the heart of Andie's smarter work program. As we have seen, Billie's work program — with all its disastrous social conse-quences — is precisely premised on the notion that he is in direct competition with his peers. This leads him to continuously intensify his efforts, while consciously working in isolation from others. One fundamental way in which Andie's work program is smarter than Billie's is that she sees her peers not as competitors but as potential collaborators. Because of this, Andie is able to take full advantage of the benefits of teamwork. Indeed, Andie firmly believes that there is truth in the acronym that is commonly generated from the word "TEAM": Together Each Achieves More. More than a mere slogan, to her it is one of the most useful pieces of advice that a law student could receive.

The reasons for this are obvious, but few people other than Andie — certainly neither Billie nor Charlie — ever stop to consider them. To begin with, Andie recognizes that the law school environ-ment leaves her surrounded by people very much like herself: in other words, *smart* people with interesting backgrounds and perspec-tives. She talks to some of these people every day about topics rang-ing from politics, sports, and other current events to the goings-on in their daily lives. When these conversations occur, she inevitably finds them both stimulating and enjoyable. And she gets the benefit of new and thoughtful perspectives on a wide array of issues. It requires no great imaginative stretch for Andie to reach the logical conclu-sion that much could be gained by talking with these people about the most obvious thing that she shares in common with them: the study of law.

The idea is so simple and obvious that one wonders why it continues to escape Billie and Charlie. Not only do such conversations offer the promise of learning from smart people with thoughtful perspectives, but the learning is also painless. In fact, it is as pleasant and enjoyable as conversations on other interesting topics that law students can be expected to have on a daily basis. Of course, there are reasons that Billie and Charlie are prevented from having this insight. The metaphorical lightbulb never turns on inside their heads because they doubt that learning law can be properly converted into a social enterprise.

For one thing, both Billie and Charlie (but especially Billie) are so focused on the zero-sum nature of the law school grading system that they cannot conceive that anything could *really* be gained by sharing one's own insights on law in exchange for the insights of others. From Billie's perspective, any attempt to organize this kind of mutual exchange of ideas is doomed to fail from the start. For it sets up a kind of "prisoner's dilemma": a situation in which one's dominant strategy is to betray the group and keep one's own best insights, regardless of what others choose to do.

After all, other members of the group will do one of two things. If others choose to share their best insights, so much the better: by betraying others, Billie will have the benefit of their ideas *and* he will get to keep his own ideas a secret (indeed, this is the best of all possible outcomes). If, on the other hand, others think as Billie does and decline to share their most insightful ideas, then he has even more incentive to betray, for now he must avoid the worst of all possible outcomes: a situation in which others have his best insights but he has none of theirs. Thus, in either case, logic seems to dictate Billie's playing it close to the vest, as it were. And because Billie knows that others can be expected to have had the same thought process, it looks as though this "social" enterprise is destined to quickly degenerate into a very antisocial and futile exercise in trying to screw the next guy.

The truly unfortunate consequence of this (as shown in the graphic) is that Billie and his like-minded cohorts end up worse-off than they would have been if they had but found some way to cooperate. Of course, Andie is no fool. She too has read Hobbes, so she knows that these kinds of dilemmas invariably threaten to interfere with any attempt to reap the benefits of social cooperation. But she

The Prisoner's Dilemma

Billie 1

	DISCLOSE	WITHHOLD
DISCLOSE	**Billie 1** › Relative advantage vis-à-vis class **Billie 2** › Relative advantage vis-à-vis class	**Billie 1** › Relative advantage vis-à-vis class › Relative advantage vis-à-vis Billie 2 **Billie 2** › Disadvantage vis-à-vis Billie 1 › Wasted time
WITHHOLD	**Billie 1** › Disadvantage vis-à-vis Billie 2 › Wasted time **Billie 2** › Relative advantage vis-à-vis class › Relative advantage vis-à-vis Billie 1	**Billie 1** › Wasted time **Billie 2** › Wasted time

Billie 2 (left vertical axis label)

also knows that such dilemmas *can* be overcome—that cooperation *is* after all possible—with a bit of *trust*. No doubt trust is a hard commodity to come by in the Hobbesian state of nature, where each is in a war against all. If Andie believed, as Billie seems to believe, that law school is just a more "civilized" version of the state of nature, she might likewise despair of finding that valuable commodity in the law school environment. But only the most hardened cynic would insist on portraying the law school environment as a Hobbesian state of nature. Some of these people are Andie's friends!

And therein lies the solution to this dilemma. For, whatever *The X-Files* might counsel, life would be a pretty poor affair — not much worth living, really — if one did not trust one's friends. Does this not suggest that a successful study group *can* be formed with friends? Andie knows that her friends are not going to hold out on her and they likewise know that she will not hold out on them. Indeed, friendship alters the basic structure of incentives that the prisoner's dilemma sets up by assuring that no one need concern himself or herself with the worst-case scenario. Friendship is, in fact, premised on cooperation. To be a friend is to be concerned with what is best for "us" instead of what is strictly best for "me"; it is to be a "we"-sayer rather than an "I"-sayer.

Because of this, Andie is confident that she and her friends can overcome, not only the desire to protect themselves against the worst possible outcome, but also any remaining perverse (egoistic) incentives for holding out. In fact, in Andie's view, those incentives were overblown to begin with. Even accepting that there are only so many As to go around, who's to say that she and her friends cannot each secure one for themselves? To be in competition with other students in the class *as a group* is not yet to be in competition with any student (or subgroup of students) in particular. Indeed, given that Andie and her friends are among a select few who know how to secure the real benefits of cooperation, it would not at all be surprising to see each and every one of them outperform the class on average.

But even if this were not true, there would be other compelling reasons for Andie and her friends to cooperate. For one thing, studying in a group with friends converts what might otherwise be an exercise in drudgery into a highly enjoyable social experience. No doubt this claim will raise the eyebrows of both Billie and Charlie, but only because they do not properly understand what group study entails.

To Charlie, studying is just studying. Whether it is done alone or in a group, it is to be avoided for the simple reason that it is not very pleasant. Andie thinks otherwise. Again, group study is not all that far removed from interesting conversation with intelligent and informed people. Surely Charlie does not want to deny that pleasure can be derived from such conversation? Indeed, law students of all stripes—including Charlie—have such conversations every day. Why should law not be the topic of these conversations?

One soon discovers, when one does make law the topic of conversation, that the study of law can become almost addictive. Andie and her friends take great joy in participating in the kind of discussion and debate that is at the heart of the public legal culture. They have genuine interest in the intellectual heritage that has been passed down to them in landmark judgments and in the legal literature. They consider themselves the beneficiaries of this heritage and its willing keepers. There is nothing overly romantic in this view: indeed, Andie believes that she and her friends react to the study of law in the way that is most natural, the way that other students would react if they brought the same enthusiasm to the study of law that they bring to their daily conversations.

Such enthusiasm gets generated all the more easily because Andie is joined by friends in her study of law. If nothing else, this helps to break up the dreary loneliness that attends Billie's approach to the study of law. But it is more than just that: for any company—even the company of strangers—would be better than none at all. Her friends are not merely strangers. These are people whose company she values in any case. Truth be told, time spent with her friends can be quite enjoyable even when they sit around doing essentially nothing. It is made all the more enjoyable when they spend their time together pursuing one of their most basic common interests.

Because of this, Andie is able to spend a great deal of time studying law. There is no sense in which her social life need interfere with studying, or vice-versa. In a very real sense, the study of law just *is* part of Andie's social life. The two are integrated so entirely that it is difficult to know where the one ends and the other begins. When Andie and her friends are not actually in class getting lectured on law, they are likely to be found in the local pub discussing the legal issues that arose in class that day over lunch or a beer. Is this studying? Certainly. But it is also socializing. Mixed in with conversations about law will be playful (not to say childish) banter, as well as discussions on all those other topics that are at the heart of our daily social interactions: sports, movies, music, politics, even gossip. Is this socializing? Of course. But because law, which Andie and her friends find at least as interesting a topic as these others, is either the immediate focus of conversation or never far from being so, it is also studying.

Andie Places a Premium on Synthesis and Unity in the Study of Law

Billie may well respond to all that we have just said with a dismissive snort. If so, he will be objecting on grounds that are more or less the converse of Charlie's: where Charlie doubts that studying can actually be pleasurable, Billie is convinced that nothing so pleasurable could *really* be considered studying. For him, studying consists of poring over reams of pages in an effort to sift out all the various details — the bits of legal trivia or minutia — that he will pound into his head and later blurt out on a final exam. The company of others is of little assistance in this regard: it is all about hard work and brute memorization. Nor should one bemoan this state of affairs. After all, Billie believes that without pain there can be no gain. The fact that Andie and her friends actually enjoy "studying" is proof that what they are doing is unworthy of that description.

Of course, if Billie were right about the definition of "studying," then he would also be right to think that Andie and her friends are doing nothing of the sort. There is no sense in which they spend countless hours at the pub each day playing some law-specific version of Trivial Pursuit (though even this might be preferable to what Billie does). Throughout most of the semester, Andie and her friends remain as unconcerned about the minutia of the numerous cases they are asked to read as they are about how many U.S. states have names beginning with the letter "W."

The reason for this is quite simple: Billie's definition of "studying" is far too narrow. Details of the cases are no doubt important, and at some point — usually in the days immediately preceding the exam — Andie will spend time alone getting very intimate with those details (though we will see that, even then, there are ways in which she can work together with her friends to minimize the loneliness involved). But in the meantime, there is no reason to suppose

23

that useful studying cannot be done without thorough knowledge of such details. That supposition could only be based on the unspoken premise that law is nothing more than an agglomeration of discrete and disconnected facts and rulings. Billie may be prepared to accept that premise uncritically, but it is one that Andie is keen to reject.

This in fact is another fundamental way in which Andie's work program is smarter than Billie's. For, Andie realizes that the easiest way to master a set of details (whether legal or otherwise) is to see them as interrelated parts of an integrated whole. To take a rather crude example, when shopping for groceries, one is far less likely to forget items on one's mental checklist if—instead of simply being told to purchase eggs, flour, baking powder, vegetable oil, butter, sugar, cocoa, *et cetera*—one is told that the items are being purchased to bake a chocolate cake. Knowing that one is baking a cake lends a *synthetic unity*, or a *systematic coherence*, to the items on the list. One is able to think of the ingredients in connection with one another, making it much more probable that no single ingredient will be overlooked.

Being able to synthesize, or give systematic unity to, a set of details also helps one to master them in ways that go beyond mere mnemonics. One *understands* something about the ingredients on one's mental checklist if one knows that one is baking a chocolate cake. For starters, one understands that those ingredients go together in a way that is exclusive of other items like, say, Tabasco sauce. Only the most ardent fan of spice would think to add Tabasco sauce to his chocolate cake: to most of us, this would not only seem incongruous, but directly inimical to the cake's intended sweetness. Thus, the unifying concept "chocolate cake" imposes a constraint of *fit* on one's mental checklist, making it improbable that one will mistakenly expand the list by adding incongruous elements.

Similarly, it makes one aware of differences in the relative significance of specific items on the list. Absent such a unifying concept, one would have no special reason to suppose that cocoa, for example, was any more important to the list than vegetable oil: all items on one's checklist would seem equally (in)significant. But because one knows that one is baking a chocolate cake, one realizes that vegetable oil (which merely performs the function of making the cake moist) can be replaced by mayonnaise, or perhaps left off the list altogether, whereas cocoa (which performs the function of making the cake chocolaty) is both an indispensable and irreplaceable item on the list. Likewise, one surmises that flour may be even more important to the list than cocoa. For, without cocoa one could still bake a cake (though certainly not a *chocolate* cake), but how would one go about doing so without flour? The unifying concept "chocolate cake" (or, more generally, "cake") thus allows one to sort the various items on one's mental checklist in ways that would not otherwise be possible.

So much so, in fact, that one could quite reasonably neglect to form any mental checklist whatsoever, and simply walk into a grocery store with the idea of buying the ingredients for a "chocolate cake," without necessarily being any worse off for it. So long as one understood that one needed certain items to form a basic batter (milk, flour, eggs), some to make the cake rise (baking powder), some to make it moist (vegetable oil), some to lend it flavour and sweetness (cocoa, sugar), and so forth, one could pretty well be assured of leaving the store with all the necessary items. In other words, by understanding the unifying concept "cake" and how a cake is put together — how its ingredients relate to one another — one can reasonably forego detailed knowledge of the ingredients themselves (at least in the short term). These details can always be derived or slotted in later by relying on one's more general understanding of how cakes work. Indeed, this is one of the greatest benefits of using unifying concepts to sort details.

As with "cake" (or "chocolate cake"), so with "law" (or whatever more specific field of law one cares to name). Andie knows that by approaching law as a systematic discipline, one whose details can be synthesized under unifying concepts and categories, she can gain a strong understanding of those details and how they fit together, without necessarily focusing on the details themselves. Billie fails to see how studying can be pleasurable only because he approaches law as though he were memorizing detailed and disconnected items on a grocery list. No doubt this is dreary work, and one's friends are unlikely to be of much assistance in doing such work. But because Andie and her friends focus their conversations on bigger questions — the legal equivalents of how a cake (or a chocolate cake) is put together — there is no sense in which studying must be dreary and lonely for them. After all, these bigger questions are interesting and theoretically taut in a way that no exercise in mere memorization can be; they call for consultation and debate where memorization calls only for concentration and solitude.

And because of the benefits of using unifying concepts, Andie's method of studying is not only more enjoyable than Billie's: it is ultimately more successful. Andie learns more than mere details such as case names, the facts of those cases, and their holdings. She also learns how those cases hang together; thus, she learns to identify cases that are incongruous, or that do not quite *fit*, with the rest of the case law. She learns which cases are most *indispensable* or *irreplaceable* to an area of law in the sense that they stand for core principles. In short, she learns all that one learns about the items in a grocery list by being able to unify them under the concept "chocolate cake." Moreover, just as in the example, she learns all this without needing to concern herself too much with the details themselves, secure in the knowledge that she will eventually be able to slot those details into her unified system of understanding, both effortlessly and in a way that ensures that they will not easily be forgotten when they are actually needed: on an exam.

The question now becomes: How is all this possible? Where does Andie come by these unifying concepts and categories that help her to synthesize or systematize legal details? A great deal of ink has been spilt by legal academics on the issue of whether law is actually instinct with such concepts and categories, whether it has underlying principles and ideas that, like the concept of "chocolate cake" in our grocery list example, can help one to synthesize its details.

That issue is largely a matter of indifference to Andie. It makes not a jot of difference to her, from the standpoint of doing well academically (and with a minimum of effort), whether her unifying concepts are actually immanent in the law or whether they are imposed from without. In either case, a great deal can be gained by using such unifying concepts. Similarly, if through some happy coincidence it turned out that the items on her grocery list exactly matched those needed to bake a chocolate cake, Andie would not let the fact that those items were never *intended* to bake a cake—that the concept "cake" was not *immanent* or *instinct* in the list itself—stop her from using that concept to sort the various details on the list. For, even in that case, she could derive the benefits of doing so. In fact, Andie might even go so far as to invent such a unifying concept herself, if one did not immediately suggest itself, and impose it on her list *after the fact,* in order to be able to reap these benefits.

This is not to suggest that Andie is *entirely* indifferent to which unifying concept (or set of concepts) she uses to synthesize detail. She recognizes, to be sure, that some are better than others. Any attempt to unify the items on our grocery list under the concept "lasagna" would no doubt meet with Andie's disapproval. Such a concept would fail to "fit" the phenomena, it would not cohere with the details themselves and so could be of little help in understanding them. Thus, Andie recognizes "fit" as the most basic criterion by which any good set of unifying concepts must be judged. Indeed, to the extent that a set of concepts achieves almost perfect fit with the details themselves, Andie may even be tempted to think that they are immanent in those details. She may think, for example, that the concept "chocolate cake" is immanent in our grocery list example, that such a happy marriage of concept and detail could not simply be an accident. Regardless, Andie will always prefer concepts that achieve greater fit to those that achieve less, whether one is talking about grocery lists or legal phenomena.

From the perspective of achieving academic success, however, Andie knows that there is another essential characteristic of unifying concepts that is even more important than "fit." That is, *they must match the preferred theoretical approach to law of her professors.* If Andie were taking a course in grocery shopping and her professor believed that the items on our mental checklist could best be unified under the concept "cookie" (Andie takes it for granted that even the most unreflective professor would not try to unify those items under a concept as alien to them as "lasagna"), then Andie would do her best to try to understand the items in the light of that concept. Her study sessions with friends would mainly consist of discussions surrounding how cookies are put together, what the function of their various ingredients are, and how those ingredients interrelate. This is so even though she and her friends might secretly harbour a belief that the concept "cake" did a better job of unifying the items on the list, or achieved a better "fit" with the details themselves. Of course, in that case, they might still spend *some* time trying to understand the details of the list under their own preferred concept (especially where the professor's preferred concept left certain details unexplained), but for the most part they would be working with the concept "cookie" rather than the concept "cake."

There is nothing unduly deferential or obsequious in this. Andie's behaviour in this regard is merely properly *strategic*. Indeed, this is one further respect in which Andie's work program is fundamentally smarter than Billie's. In all she does, Andie is attuned to the fact that her ultimate goal is to *achieve a good grade* with as little effort as possible. And since it is her professors who will ultimately make the determination of what grade she should receive, Andie goes out of her way to not only become acquainted with her professors' favoured approaches to law but to become quite conversant in them and adopt them herself for the purposes of completing graded work.

Billie, by way of contrast, fails to even take notice of the differences in his professors' favoured theoretical approaches to law. Instead, he tends to treat all graded exercises as though they were being completed for one type of professor in particular (whose acquaintance we will presently make). The fault here lies in Billie's familiar tacit assumption that law (not to mention the typical grocery list) consists only of discrete and disconnected details, embodied in particular rules and cases. His graded work reflects this assumption. This may not hurt Billie when he is being graded by a professor who shares his assumption, but it is bound to recoil on him when he is being graded by a professor who does not. To a grocery-shopping professor who thinks that the items on our grocery list are best understood as being unified by the concept "cookie," any exam on the contents of that list that fails to reflect this understanding can only seem woefully incomplete. Billie's treatment of the items as discrete and disconnected will appear to that professor to have missed out on the *essence* of the list, however accurate his description of its detailed contents might be. So too in the case of law professors: failure to reflect an understanding of their preferred approach to law in one's graded work can only be seen by them as failure to appreciate the essence of law.

Nor would Billie be likely to meet with greater success if his exam answer were guided by a *reasoned belief*, rather than an unspoken assumption, that law consists only of discrete and disconnected details. Again, for her part Andie may well think that the items on our grocery list are more appropriately understood by reference to the concept "cake" than by reference to the concept "cookie."

However, if her professor thinks otherwise, she is not going to debate this point with him on an exam that he is grading. She may (and often will) privately refer to her own preferred unifying concept for the purposes of bettering her personal understanding, but for the purposes of writing an exam it is his preferred concept that she will reference.

If others consider this to be blatant pandering to professorial prejudice, then so be it. In Andie's view, the truth is that professorial "prejudice" does not even enter into the equation. Instead, Andie realizes that her professor has had the benefit of considerably more time to think about the area of law he is teaching. Indeed, he has probably been teaching in that area for years, whereas this may well be her first exposure to it. Thus, unless she is prepared to conclude that she is much smarter than her professor (and Andie tries to avoid being guilty of intellectual hubris), she is generally willing to give him the benefit of the doubt that he is better situated to determine which theoretical approach to that area of law is best.

Of course, if Andie feels very strongly about the issue, she may decide to publish her views in the school's law review. But trying to point out the error of her professor's ways in an exam by giving an extended treatise on why her approach to law is preferable can only be a losing proposition. Again, unless she thinks especially highly of her powers of argument, Andie is well aware that he has probably heard similar arguments in the past and, for whatever reason, found them wanting. Rather than try to fight this losing battle, Andie will therefore ensure that what she communicates in her work is being received by as receptive an audience as possible. This entails adopting the professor's preferred theoretical approach to law, however distasteful Andie might find it. For Andie knows that, in the end, human nature is such that people in general—and professors in particular—cannot help but be most impressed by those views that they happen to already share.

Our Supporting Cast: Knowing the Professors

In what remains of this chapter we will try to give the reader a sense of the different theoretical approaches to law that Andie can expect to come across in her dealings with various professors over the course of her law school career. Each general *type* of approach is embodied below in a *type* of professor, whom we have affectionately named after an occupational counterpart in some other field who shares his interests. There are four such types: The Philosopher, The Politician, The Economist, and Doctor Doctrine.

We cannot overstress that these are merely general "Types." Within each type, Andie comes across a great many subtypes (and sub-subtypes). There are as many ways to be The Politician, for example, as there are professors who prefer this approach to law. We cannot catalogue all the various subtypes. That is why we will endeavour only to give the reader a "sense" of the different approaches, highlighting their main features as well as some of the more endearing idiosyncrasies one might find in the professors who adopt them.

We further caution the reader that not all professors are *easily* classifiable under this taxonomy. Some overlap exists between the types, with the result that a professor who shares certain characteristics with, say, The Philosopher may, on further inspection, turn out to be The Politician. This may cause some initial confusion. However, with practice and experience (and considerable care in exercising one's judgment), one will find that one's ability to accurately classify professors will eventually match Andie's.

The rewards for reaching this level of proficiency will be well worth the effort, for reasons that have already been discussed but will soon be expanded upon. Indeed, knowing her professors is on par with teamwork and synthesis in terms of its importance to Andie's systematic approach to law school: it is, as the title of this chapter suggests, one of the major building blocks of that approach.

The Philosopher

Of all Andie's professors, The Philosopher may be the most easily identifiable on the basis of appearance and mannerisms alone. He often looks the part: white hair growing in all directions atop a furrowed brow, perhaps a beard or eyeglasses, and clothes that are practical if not quite the height of fashion. He sometimes acts the part: showing up to class ten minutes late and mumbling an apology (something about losing track of time) while staring distractedly at his watch. And, in some instances, he may even sound the part:

using long, drawn-out sentences that consist largely of a string of "hmmms" punctuated by the occasional "uh."

But do not let any of this distract you from the fact that he is to be taken seriously. Andie takes him extremely seriously. She understands that if he sometimes fails to keep the little details in order—things like his personal appearance, his punctuality, or the eloquence of his speech—it is only because his mind is focused on matters of far greater importance. In fact, Andie considers The Philosopher to be engaged in an exercise very similar to her own: systematizing the law in search of greater knowledge and understanding of its various components.

Other professors, it is true, also seek to impose their own kind of order and unity on the body of cases and doctrines that comprise the law, but only The Philosopher searches for that unity merely for the sake of understanding or knowledge itself. That is what makes him deserving of the name "Philosopher": for he is truly a lover of knowledge. Unlike others, he sees in Law (the capitalization here is no mistake; in his eyes the term is deserving of nothing less) a self-standing discipline demanding respect and careful study for reasons quite apart from any instrumental benefits its understanding might yield. To him, there is a kind of conceptual purity, or beauty, or elegance in Law that is the product of sustained effort by many great thinkers, across tens of generations, to carefully work out a system of public reason.

Because of this, it is more appropriate to view The Philosopher as one who "searches" for unity in Law, rather than one who "imposes" unity on the law. Indeed, The Philosopher is the most likely of all professors to think that Law has its own set of immanent unifying concepts. As he sees it, his task is to find the common threads or the recurring themes that tie together the efforts of others over time to publicly articulate the ideas and concepts for which Law itself is constantly groping, towards which it is forever striving. This vision gives rise to two fundamental characteristics that are at the core of the Philosopher's identity (and should thus be of great assistance in picking him out).

First, because of his focus on Law's immanent *structure*, and his concern for the *themes* that run through Law, The Philosopher is likely to display more commitment to ideals of *consistency* and *coherence* than other types of professors. That is, he is likely to reject any form of legal reasoning—including any he finds in decided cases at the "fringes" of law (for that is where he will inevitably relegate them)—that does not properly fit this structure, or runs against the grain of Law's recurring themes.

Second, albeit not entirely distinct, because The Philosopher believes that Law has *its own* unity, he will be hostile to any attempt to impose a different unity on it from without. This means, in the first instance, that he is averse to all efforts to understand law instrumentally, or in terms of any prospective good it can accomplish. Such efforts entail attempting to unify law according to what it *should* or *could* be, rather than according to what it *is*. In connection with this, The Philosopher will disdain any attempt to pollute legal reasoning with the sorts of considerations that generally fall under the rubric of "policy." Unless these policy concerns are already latent within the structure of Law (in which case they are better viewed as matters of legal principle than as matters of "policy"), their intrusion on our attempts to reason about Law can only interfere with Law's own aspirations for itself.

The Philosopher is sometimes accused of being politically conservative as a result of this resistance to seeing Law used as an instrument for the advancement of politically progressive policies. In reality, his politics need never enter into things. The Philosopher may well be as progressive as the next person (whether he is, in the end, is his business alone). His only necessary conservatism is with respect to Law itself: he will not see it changed in the name of political progress; any changes to Law must be mandated by its own internal structure and principles.

All of which raises the question of what The Philosopher sees those principles to be. In other words, what unifying concepts are immanent to Law? As we explained at the beginning of this section, there is a wide range of possible variance here: he may see Law as a system of individual *right*; or, quite the contrary, he may see it as a system that implements *communitarian* ideals. Between these poles there are any number of possibilities. The best way to pin down The Philosopher's—or, for that matter, any professor's—precise views is to listen attentively to what he says in class and spend some time after class reading his published work (in the next chapter we will discuss how time can be freed up in order to do this without necessarily increasing one's overall workload).

Finally, we caution the reader against making hasty assumptions that one has come across The Philosopher on the basis of the language that he uses. Although it is true that The Philosopher's speech is often replete with normatively laden terms like "rights," "justice," or "utility," such terms are not exclusive to him. As we will see, The Politician also speaks in terms of (human) "rights" and (social) "justice," and the language of "utility" is not unknown to The Economist. In the end, the best way to identify The Philosopher is not on the basis of his forms of expression, but on the basis of those fundamental characteristics discussed above.

The Politician

In many ways, The Politician is the antithesis of The Philosopher. Where The Philosopher often looks unkempt, The Politician's suit will likely be freshly pressed. Where The Philosopher can appear distracted, The Politician invariably seems sharp. And, most importantly, where The Philosopher sometimes sacrifices eloquence in search of the precise term he needs to express his ideas, The Politician's speech always seems smooth and effortless.

This can all be attributed to the fact that The Politician is essentially a kind of public advocate or lobbyist. In order to help persuade others of the worthiness of his favoured causes, he seeks to create a favourable impression on them with his appearance, his manner, and especially his speech. This focus on advocacy signals a marked departure from The Philosopher's approach to Law. For it is premised on the notion that the law can and should be shaped in furtherance of whatever causes The Politician advocates. In turn, this premise implicitly embraces the very ideas that The Philosopher rejects: that law should be understood both *instrumentally* as a powerful tool for social engineering and, more specifically, that it should be understood in terms of its role in advancing one's preferred *policies*.

In The Politician's case, those policies can most often be captured under the broad heading "social justice". Whether this gets cashed out in terms of workers' rights, women's rights, aboriginal rights, or human rights more generally (and it is quite probable that The Politician will champion social justice in all these various forms), the general approach to law is the same. Legal decisions are to be considered prospectively, and analyzed retrospectively, according to whether they are consistent with, or help to further, the chosen policies. Such policies are the unifying concepts in The Politician's approach to law.

Of course, this approach to the law entails a wholesale rejection of virtually all that The Philosopher holds dear, which is not surprising, given that it relies on the sort of instrumentalist reasoning that he despises. Whereas The Philosopher places a premium on consistency and coherence within Law itself, The Politician is likely to scoff at these ideals. If past decisions do not adequately reflect the importance of The Politician's preferred social policies, so much the worse for legal coherence: the law should be set on an entirely new and different course. Indeed, the only consistency that The Politician values is a kind of forward-looking consistency in implementing the necessary changes to legal doctrine.

In support of his rejection of legal coherence, The Politician will likely even go as far as to dispute The Philosopher's more basic claim that Law has its own set of internal principles (or unifying concepts) that govern and constrain the ways in which the law should be developed. His attack on this claim will be two-pronged. First, he will deny that legal principles have the kind of universality and general application that The Philosopher wants to claim for them. Indeed, The Politician will emphasize *contextual analysis* of legal problems as a way of limiting the reach of legal principle. Different contexts, he will say, call for different legal responses to problems, and no unyielding principle is suited to providing the required flexibility of response.

Second, and more radically, The Politician may even deny that the unifying concepts and principles that The Philosopher claims to have found within Law itself are the law's "own" principles. Even assuming that the legal tradition is instinct with such principles, there is no sense in which the ones The Philosopher has fixed on are there exclusively. Instead, the law consists of a congeries of different — often directly opposed and competing — principles. Because he focuses on some of these to the exclusion of others, The Philosopher's claim to have "discovered" a unity in Law is partial. There are many other different unities he might have "discovered" by focusing instead on different principles. Thus, what The Philosopher identifies as Law's "own" unity is actually constructed by him: it is, in other words, as externally imposed as any other unity.

From these premises, only a short logical step is required in order to reach The Politician's ultimate conclusion. What The Philosopher passes off as adherence to principle, or coherence, is merely his own brand of conservative politics masquerading as such. The idea that there are unique legal principles, and that these principles should bind us in all circumstances, merely serves to reinforce the political status quo. But if the status quo is to be preserved, then that determination should be made, not in The Philosopher's study under the opaque (and protective) cover of highfalutin appeal to principle, but out in the open, in the political arena of which law forms a constitutive part. Hence the Politician's focus on advocacy: he is certain that he can persuade the public legal culture to join his cause once the political debate is properly framed as such.

It should be clear from all this, if it was not already, that deep theory is not the exclusive domain of The Philosopher. The Politician also relies heavily on abstract theoretical thought. Indeed, the deconstruction of The Philosopher's approach to law that we have just described can be credited to one form of politician in particular: the critical legal theorist (legal theory's answer to the postmodernist). There are a number of other theories of which The Politician may also choose to avail himself: from feminist theory, to difference theory, to sociology. One should not assume, then, that one is encountering The Philosopher merely because a professor is a theoretician. Where theory is invoked for the sake of clearing space for political debate in the legal context (as in the case of the critical legal theorist), or for the sake of establishing the importance and worthiness of certain political causes (as in the case of these other theories), rather than for the sake of understanding Law itself as a discrete and self-standing discipline (which is how The Philosopher claims to use theory), it is probable that one has come across The Politician instead.

The Economist

It would not be far from the truth to say that The Economist is a kind of hybrid politician/philosopher. Like The Politician, The

Economist understands law as a tool for the advancement of certain goals (indeed most conservative politicians tend to fall into the economist camp). In the case of The Economist, however, those goals tend to be economic rather than social in nature. Thus, the law is for him an instrument directed at achieving "wealth maximization" or increasing the economic "efficiency" of social transactions. These are the core values — or, to use our preferred language, the unifying concepts — of The Economist's approach to law.

It is typically quite easy to spot The Economist simply by virtue of the fact that his linguistic patterns scream out his commitment to these unifying concepts. Indeed, the term "efficiency" seems to roll off of his tongue with the frequency and ease of water rolling off an umbrella. Among the other pet terms and phrases that comprise his lexicon (and instantly give him away) are the following: "transaction costs," "lowest cost avoider," "cost externalization," "free-rider problem," "informational asymmetry," "loss distribution," "risk distribution," and "rational agency" (to name but a few). Unfortunately, all this jargon, while making The Economist easy to identify, poses problems of its own.

For one thing, it can make his approach to law seem esoteric and opaque. Explaining all his terminology would, of course, be beyond the scope of this book. Suffice it to say, however, that each of these terms is in some way directed to further articulating The Economist's core unifying concept of "efficiency." Here, as before, we refer the reader to The Economist's published work, and to his classroom discussion, in order to get a better sense of what these various terms mean (including "efficiency" itself, which is a term of art with potentially ambiguous meaning for The Economist).

Perhaps even more disconcerting than the obscurity of The Economist's language is that it appears, at first blush, to be completely divorced from the language of law itself. One can easily imagine how The Philosopher's — or, for that matter, The Politician's — references to "rights" and "justice" might be relevant for the purposes of legal analysis: for these are terms that are quite native to law. But what of references to such concepts as "risk aversion" or "diminishing marginal utility"? What do any of *these* concepts have to do with law?

From The Economist's perspective, the answer is likely to be "everything!" In fact, most variants of The Economist believe that these concepts are the law's *own* unifying concepts, that they drive the law's evolution inasmuch as they both underlie and animate more familiar legal concepts, which merely stand in as popular analytical surrogates for them. This, of course, is just another way of saying that such concepts are immanent (albeit deeply so) in the structure of law itself. In saying this, moreover, The Economist betrays a kind of loose affiliation with The Philosopher. This will manifest itself most obviously in The Economist's concern for systematic implementation of the concept of efficiency, and his disavowal of the relevance of what he considers to be other "extraneous" considerations.

Doctor Doctrine

We have consciously saved for last our discussion of Doctor Doctrine, if only because he sits uneasily within our taxonomy. Our goal throughout has been to identify the basic theoretical approaches to law of various professors. The problem with Doctor Doctrine is that he lacks such an approach.

To be sure, Doctor Doctrine shares, at some level, certain characteristics with other professors. He believes along with The Philosopher, for example, that law is a self-standing discipline that is deserving of study for its own sake. But whereas The Philosopher seeks to understand Law as a coherent system of public reason, Doctor Doctrine is more or less content to understand it as a body of discrete doctrines and rulings. Whereas The Philosopher is likely to devote his time to writing theoretical treatises, Doctor Doctrine is the most likely of all professors to produce a basic textbook that simply collects and catalogues cases under discrete headings.

Not surprisingly, his remarkable breadth of doctrinal knowledge (to which his textbooks stand as testament) is perhaps the best way to identify Doctor Doctrine. And because his knowledge is so broad, it should also come as no surprise that this leaves little time for exploring any single idea in great depth. He may dabble in theory in the course of class discussion, but because his forays into this area are both sporadic and inconsistent (he takes a bit from the approaches of all his colleagues) it is clear that he views theory as an interesting sidebar rather than as something at the core of law.

As a result of all this, Doctor Doctrine poses a special problem for Andie. For, in classes with him, her relative strengths are deemphasized. There is little room for synthetic unity, or systematic understanding in a class taught by Doctor Doctrine: here as always, Andie adopts the preferred theoretical approach of her professor, even when that entails abandoning theory for the purposes of completing graded work. Indeed, Doctor Doctrine's class is where Billie is likely to be most at home. After all, it provides him with a venue to display his encyclopedic knowledge of legal trivia to a willing and interested audience.

Saying all this, there are basic strategies that Andie can implement even in Doctor Doctrine's class to ensure that she need not travel down the long dreary road to Billiedom. In the chapters that follow, we shall outline these strategies among others.

A Note on Heuristics

Terminology

Throughout this book, we use certain expressions with which the reader is likely to be unfamiliar. Two of these expressions, in particular, require explanation inasmuch as their meaning is central to both the structure of this book and its mode of presentation. The first — "Shoe" — is a rough proximate for what others sometimes refer to as "myth." The second — "Big Bill" — similarly approximates the meaning of the term "tip." We prefer our language, not only because it is more colourful, but also because it contains additional layers of meaning.

The Origin of the Shoe

This term has its genesis in an experience we had while we were in our second year of law school. We were preparing for a moot (a kind of formal debate, only in the legal context), which set us the task of arguing both sides of a well-defined legal problem. After discussing the problem among ourselves for some time, we reached the conclusion that it did not present an arguable legal issue. Therefore, we approached our faculty advisor, who was charged with helping us to sort out these sorts of difficulties. Unfortunately, he failed to see the source of our concern. Instead, he lectured us at length on what he took to be the intricacies of the legal issue. At this point, one of us replied in puzzlement, "I don't know how you're seeing a *real* issue here—to us, it looks completely one-sided. It's a slam dunk!" We did not even have time to elucidate, for on hearing this, our professor's face lit up. "I'd never thought of it like that before!" he exclaimed. He jumped out of his seat and began flipping through a textbook he had on his shelf in an effort to get to the bottom of the difficulty we had brought to his attention.

Later, we were laughing about how excited our professor had become in response to this comment. It was apparent that the source of his excitement was not any argument we had put forth—again, his reaction pre-empted any attempt on our part to buttress our claim with argument. Rather, he seemed excited by our use of the expression "slam dunk." It was as though he had been bowled over by the mere invocation of this image. This reminded us of an episode of *The Simpsons* we had all seen.

In the episode, Homer was betting on the outcome of football games. He was watching TV, flipping channels, when he came across a prognosticator offering his "picks." The prognosticator— "Smooth" Jimmy Apollo—predicted that Miami was a "lock" to beat Cincinnati in his game of the week. For emphasis, he held up an oversized padlock as he said this. Homer, seemingly convinced by this visual pun, exclaimed, "That's a big lock!" He then turned to another channel, where a different prognosticator was in the midst of assuring viewers that Cincinnati was a "shoo-in" to beat Miami. As he said this he held up a giant shoe. This caused Homer to doubt his initial assessment: "They both make good arguments," he mused with a quizzical look on his face.

As we saw it, our professor had responded to the expression "slam dunk" in much the same way that Homer had responded to "lock" and "shoe". In both cases, the form of the expression was enough to convince without any reference to substantive argument. Hence, the word "shoe" became synonymous with emphatic and unsubstantiated declarations that seek to impress and convince by the mere force with which they are conveyed.

Throughout this book, we uncover the sort of "shoes" that are prevalent around law school. This task is analogous to debunking myth to the extent that shoes and myths share the quality of being impressive-sounding but untrue. In our view, however, law school shoes are even more insidious than the typical myth. They have a self-validating quality for those who espouse them. When Billie, for example, tells us that "law school is more difficult than anything we have ever faced before," this has the effect of stroking his own ego and affirming his sense of himself as a hard-working individual. Given this seductive quality, shoes are both easier to fall for and harder to rid oneself of than many myths.

The Origin of the Big Bill

"Big Bill" is another term that came out of our law school experience. The term was inspired by a paper we read that was written by the noted development economist, Mancur Olson. Olson relates a tale that goes something like this. If two economists walking down the street were to come across some money lying on a well-travelled sidewalk, they would refuse to pick it up. For them, the money could not exist. After all, if it did exist, somebody else would long ago have stooped over to pick it up. Thus, Olson's hypothetical economists walk by, leaving the money for someone else.

For us, the term "Big Bill" has come to signify any obvious truth whose existence is nevertheless either overlooked or consciously denied. In the law school context, the idea that there are no Big Bills lying on the sidewalk is implicit in the received wisdom. This received wisdom posits that in law school there are no shortcuts and no substitutes for hard work. Therefore, there is no such thing as "found money". Indeed, a proponent of such a view might query: If the system described in this book is so superior, why are so few people implementing it?

The response to this question lies partly in Olson's hypothetical tale, and partly in the prevalence of Shoes around law school. Most people fail to pick up the wealth of Big Bills that are left lying around the law school hallway (or sidewalk, if you prefer) because they refuse to believe in them. This refusal is directly related to the attractiveness of Shoes, which constitute much of the received wisdom. Because so many people are validated by the idea that there are no shortcuts in law school—no substitutes for hard work—their own self-image interferes with their ability to believe in Big Bills. In other words, the belief in Shoes requires one to disavow the existence of the sorts of Big Bills that are described throughout this book. This results in a phenomenon that is akin to what economists sometimes call a "market failure". Because students "buy into" shoes at the expense of buying into Big Bills, there is an overconsumption of the one "good" (if it can even be called that) at the expense of the other. For the person seeking to attain a wealth of good grades while concurrently maximizing her enjoyment of life, this market failure must be overcome.

The connection between "Big Bills" and "Tips" should be apparent. They are different, however, in the sense that Big Bills are more likely to inspire some resistance on the part of our reader (because of their antithetical relationship to Shoes).

Our Sample Case: *Hadley* v. *Baxendale*

There remains one final matter that needs to be addressed. The purpose of this book is to suggest a strategic approach to law school that can be deployed from day one. A good pedagogical technique in this regard is to teach by example. The problem here is that we must assume that our reader has no background in the law and no knowledge of any substantive doctrine. Thus, teaching by example is difficult. After all, how does one explain a systematic approach to legal study without any reference to the material being studied? It is necessary, then, to develop some minimal knowledge of doctrine. To be sure, not much is required. Accordingly, we will rely on a single case and its accompanying doctrine, deploying it throughout to show how Andie and her two foils develop their understanding of the law and, ultimately, how Andie uses the understanding thus generated to answer a final exam based on this case. In this way, we will help the reader to develop a set of skills that she will be able to use in the context of any given collection of doctrine as embodied in a single course.

The case we use is *Hadley* v. *Baxendale*, the full text of which is located in an appendix to this book. It is a venerable contract law case that addresses the doctrine of "Consequential Loss" and has received careful and persistent consideration throughout the common law world. The case involved the following facts. The plaintiff, a miller, broke a crankshaft and needed a new one made. The manufacturer of the new shaft required the broken shaft as a pattern for the new one, and the plaintiff contracted with the defendant carrier to deliver the broken shaft to the manufacturer. The defendant was late in delivering the shaft, and as a result, the plaintiff's mill was without a shaft and remained idle. The upshot of this was that the plaintiff lost profits that he would have otherwise made had the mill been in operation. The plaintiff sued the defendant for these lost profits.

In refusing to award the plaintiff damages for lost profits, the court stated the following rule: if a defendant fails to perform a contract, he is only liable to pay for those losses that could ordinarily be expected to arise from his failure to perform. The time that is relevant to this analysis is the time at which the contract was formed. Any other losses will be seen as "special" in that they result from the plaintiff's particular circumstances. The defendant is required to pay for special losses only where the plaintiff actually communicated the risk of these losses to the defendant at the time of contract formation.

Put succinctly, the rule in this case embodies the principle that the defendant is liable only for those losses that were reasonably foreseeable at the time the contract was formed. There are two types of loss that will be reasonably foreseeable: (1) ordinary loss and (2) special loss, the possibility of which was communicated to the defendant at the time the contract was formed.

In refusing to award the plaintiff damages for his lost profits, the court found that the lost profits constituted a loss that was out of the ordinary and thus "special" to the plaintiff. In the court's view, the late delivery of a shaft would not ordinarily cause a mill to stand idle. For example, the defendant might have made the reasonable assumption that the plaintiff was sending this shaft so that he could have a spare made. Since the plaintiff did not tell the defendant that the mill could not operate without the shaft, and would thus lose profits if the shaft was delivered late, the defendant could not be liable for this "special" loss.

If the meaning of this case is not entirely clear at this point, there is no cause for alarm. There will be plenty of opportunities to revisit the case. Indeed, it is expected that the reader's understanding of this case will develop as she progresses through the book. With all this in mind, it is now possible to turn to the next chapter, in which we see how each of our three characters approaches the law school semester.

two

The SEMESTER

SUPPOSE our three protagonists have decided that they want to become better basketball players. How do you think each approaches the task of improving his or her skills? Since Billie sees sweat and perseverance as the lifeblood of achievement, it should come as no surprise that he takes a disciplined and workmanlike approach. He stoically arrives at the gym each morning at 5 a.m., whereupon he commences his routine: 100 laps around the court and 200 free throws followed by eight sets of calf raises. While all this undoubtedly leaves Billie's body fitter than it has ever been, it is considerably less certain that his basketball skills will markedly improve, even after several months of following this regimen. Sadly, such a demanding routine also has the effect of making Billie's mornings the darkest part of the day.

Charlie's routine likely looks similar to Billie's, at least at first. Charlie too assumes that acquiring the skills he needs to succeed at this new endeavour requires him to exert considerable effort. Accordingly, for the first several days he too will arrive at the gym at 5 a.m. ready for shooting drills and laps. Unfortunately, Charlie is not nearly as confident as Billie. Thus, when he finds that he is labouring around the track and bricking free throws, he soon gets discouraged. He shortly foregoes his trips to the gym each morning in favour of a more indolent lifestyle that includes adequate sleep. Although Charlie's mornings will thereafter be considerably more fun-filled, he is obviously not going to improve as a basketball player. Of course, this will cause Charlie no great concern at first. Indeed, he will probably mock Billie for sacrificing so much in pursuit of what Charlie now considers to be a senseless goal. Unfortunately for Charlie, it is Billie who will have the last laugh. For when Charlie takes up the pursuit of basketball again—and he inevitably will, given that he has not always found it so "senseless"—he will find that he does not have the fitness to keep pace with Billie, who will run him ragged up and down the court.

Andie's approach to improving her basketball skills is very different from Billie's and Charlie's. For starters, she is not so accepting of the premise that sweat and toil provide the most direct route to improvement. Thus, rather than adopt a brutal workout regimen, she chooses one that is strategically engineered to improve the skills necessary to being a good basketball player. Andie realizes that while accurate shooting and physical conditioning are important, they do not exhaust—nor even get at the essence of—what is required in order to excel at basketball. Basketball involves a unique set of skills—dribbling in traffic, reading the play, rebounding—that can only be honed by practising the game itself, not some isolated component of it. In other words, she recognizes that the most direct way to become a better basketball player is to play basketball. In addition to being the shortest road to success, playing basketball also happens to be the most enjoyable way of honing one's skills. Andie takes full advantage of this happy convergence of interests, for it offers her the best of all possible worlds: she can develop the requisite skills while enjoying her life.

The beginning of a law school semester is not unlike the first day our characters arrived at the gym in the preceding hypothetical scenario. Law school is a new endeavour and requires our characters to develop a new skill set. As in the above analogy, each character will respond to this challenge in his or her own way, with varying degrees of success. Moreover, we will see that the most effective approach involves directly engaging with what is at the core of this new endeavour. Just as the best way to succeed at basketball is to play basketball, the best way to succeed at law school is to "play" the law school "game."

Class Attendance

Listening and Taking Notes

To begin seeing how the law school "game" is played, let's walk down the hall from the locker room to the classroom and see what each of our characters is up to. Charlie overslept his alarm and arrived fifteen minutes late to Contracts class. Half-asleep and day-dreaming, he is there in body but not in mind. And how could it be otherwise? Poor Charlie sits in a classroom with a professor who chucks out random bits of legal trivia. Charlie may have tried to read the cases (out of a sense of guilt if nothing else), but he was either too bored to absorb them or too overwhelmed to persevere. Now he sits in class wondering what he is supposed to be getting from it all. After class, exhausted from having "put in his time," he will have little appetite for anything to do with law school and will begin the routine anew. He will go home too tired and discouraged to read and will either scan his eyes across the pages or not bother at all. His reading "done," Charlie will call his friends — Corrie, Carrie, and Cas — and invite them over to have a few beers and watch the entire *Star Wars* tetralogy. Tomorrow he'll wake up late with little enthusiasm, arrive at class in the middle of some discussion and, being

CHARLIE'S VICIOUS CYCLE

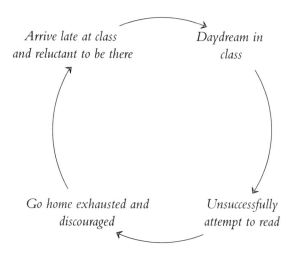

Arrive late at class
and reluctant to be there

Daydream in
class

Go home exhausted and
discouraged

Unsuccessfully
attempt to read

unable to pick up the thread, daydream to pass time. Charlie's pattern of behaviour has become a vicious cycle and it is unsurprising that his academic career is fairly unremarkable.

And what, one might ask, did Charlie miss by not paying attention in class? Well, as it happens, today the professor was discussing *Hadley v. Baxendale*, one of the key cases in all of contracts law. The discussion began with a detailed description of the facts of the case: "A miller in Gloucester contracted with a carrier to have a broken crankshaft transported to Greenwich. . . ." Frustrated with trying to get the professor's description of the facts down on the page, Charlie gave up and began to daydream. What he missed, however, was something more than just the bare essentials of the case. Although it is true that he missed the professor's description of the two-part test for recovery of consequential loss it was not necessary for him to hear even that.

The reason for this is that the facts and the doctrine can both be easily obtained elsewhere. Some Billie—either in Charlie's class or in last-year's class—will have already done the work of producing a summary of the course, wherein Charlie can easily find this information. Indeed, if Charlie were to look to his side, where Andie is seated, he would notice that she has a copy of last-year's summary in front of her and is following the discussion without having to worry about transcribing the details of the case. Charlie himself will eventually get his hands on someone else's summary (albeit too late to garner its full benefits), so it is difficult to imagine that he will walk into an exam without having a clue as to what the facts and the ruling were in *Hadley v. Baxendale*.

This brings us back to the question originally posed. What is it that Charlie missed? Unfortunately, he missed a discussion of the following important questions that were posed by the professor: "(1) How might the resolution of *Hadley v. Baxendale* be affected if the defendant was a large, well-established company like Federal Express? (2) What if the defendant offered insurance covering the goods against loss, theft, or delayed delivery? (3) What if the defendant failed to deliver the plaintiff's goods because he had been offered a higher price to deliver the goods of another person? (4) What if the mill was the only one in town, and as a result, nobody was able to buy bread?"

Every time a case is discussed, questions like these are asked, and because Andie follows the discussion of these questions, a pattern begins to emerge that helps her to identify the theory of law that her professor favours. Andie learns, for example, that The Economist is most likely to pose questions 2 and 3 (and possibly question 4) while The Politician is inclined to ask questions 1 and 4.

Moreover, she soon discovers that it is not just the questions asked, but also the answers to these questions, the language used by the professor in discussing them, and the manner in which he steers the discussion that are important for the purposes of discerning his theory. The Philosopher might pose the same questions as The Politician, but he will be posing them for a different reason: perhaps even to suggest the irrelevance of external considerations such as the greater social good. The Philosopher's interest in question 4, say, will only be to suggest that the social implications of the plaintiff's loss must be irrelevant to the assessment of damages against the defendant. "After all," he might say, "if the hardships of the plaintiff's customers are relevant, why is it that those customers are not themselves entitled to sue the defendant for breaching his contract with the plaintiff?" Or, he might ask, "Why should the plaintiff receive a windfall in the form of greater damages because she happens to be fortunate enough to have customers whose interests are aligned with her own?"

By daydreaming in class and missing discussions of this sort, Charlie loses a golden opportunity to get to know his professor. In addition, he misses the opportunity to develop his own overarching understanding of Law. Andie, meanwhile, is busy stuffing these Big Bills into her pockets. Perhaps worst of all, Charlie does not even know that he has missed these opportunities. When he does eventually get around to obtaining someone else's summary (usually at exam time), thereby acquiring the bare essentials of the case (that is, facts, issues, decision, and reasons), Charlie will assume that he has caught up to Andie. Having long since walked past a veritable mint, he will assume himself to be a Lord of infinite wealth simply because he has found a few nickels and dimes.

Billie, in contrast, appears to be Charlie's opposite in class. He has read every word that has been assigned, a fact that his colleagues can verify from his well-worn casebook, conspicuously open on his desk and highlighted in a variety of colours. Billie's book has tabbed pages and is "exam ready" almost from day one. Billie is the sort of person who furiously scribbles down each word emanating from the professor's mouth. He may even scribble down the comments of other students, although he's usually indiscriminate about this (that is, without regard for whether the comments are good or on point).

Charlie cannot help but marvel at the speed and discipline with which Billie documents the goings-on in the classroom. He wistfully envisions a trail of smoke coming from Billie's pen. And indeed, Billie's objective in class is to achieve perfect synthesis of body and pen, to become a note-taking machine. Oddly, for one who seems so interested in the goings-on in class, Billie can go weeks or even a whole semester without saying a word in class. He may be too busy writing or he may want to keep his best ideas to himself; nevertheless, he contributes very little to class discussion. When he does, it is usually to answer a question of fact. If the professor asks, "Can anyone tell me the facts of *Hadley* v. *Baxendale*?" or "In *Hadley* v. *Baxendale*, what was the plaintiff's line of work?" Billie is always the first person with his hand up.

These are questions that anyone *could* answer, but Billie shows himself to be hardworking and diligent by being one of the people who *does* answer them. As we mentioned in the introduction, one of Billie's motivations is his desire to display his extraordinary diligence, so it is not surprising that when the professor asks someone to show that he has done the reading, Billie jumps at the oppportunity. What is curious about Billie's behaviour is that when class discussion turns to questions like those raised earlier — the ones to which Charlie was completely oblivious — Billie does one of two things. On the one hand, he may transcribe every word that is said, without regard for the quality of the contribution. On the other hand, he may simply tune out. Implicit in either behaviour is a fallacious assumption that there is nothing special going on in class discussion.

This fallacious assumption is a logical consequence of Billie's approach. After all, for Billie, brute effort is all that matters. If brute effort is of no assistance in resolving questions that the professor raises for class discussion, this establishes definitively that these questions are of no importance. Accordingly, Billie rejects the utility of class discussion, assuming that his understanding will be developed by the application of still more brute effort rather than by engaging in what he believes to be "intellectual masturbation." In short, one element that is conspicuously absent from Billie's classroom strategy is a willingness to test his own ideas or tease out those of his professor by participating in the discussion of questions raised in class.

"Let's be honest, class discussion is all about students trying to show off how smart they are. I pay attention to what really matters: the professor's summary of the case."

Andie's behaviour in class superficially looks very similar to Billie's. Andie realizes that a number of important things go on in class. She also realizes that things happen quickly in the classroom, and as such, she cannot, at that very moment, sort out useful information from useless information with complete accuracy. Therefore, Andie's classroom behaviour may resemble Billie's in that both write rather furiously while class is going on.

That said, Andie's motivations for documenting the goings-on in class are very different from Billie's. While they both may scribble furiously, they will often be seen scribbling at different times. For example, when the professor discusses the facts of the case, Andie is not too worried about getting down these nuts and bolts (again, this information will be available from a summary). However, when classroom discussion begins, so does Andie's furious note-taking. But Andie's note-taking is selective. For she is always trying to discern her professor's theory. When the professor speaks about the cases, Andie thinks about whether he is a philosophical, economic, doctrinal, or political thinker. It may be difficult for Andie to classify her professor under this taxonomy at the beginning of the semester, but this changes over the course of it. As she acquires greater knowledge of the professor's theory, her classroom strategy changes. In terms of note-taking, she focuses more on those aspects of the lecture and class discussion that are relevant to the professor's theory. If Andie and Billie were fishermen, Andie would be after trophy fish while Billie would be dragging a net. Billie might come up with something worth mounting, but he is more likely to end up with a boatload of catfish and old shoes.

So what does it mean to be a trophy fisherman in class? Well, to begin with, when Andie is fishing within the pool of her professor's comments, she keeps her ear attuned to his language. For example, if her professor is The Economist, Andie's notes reflect the language of economics. They will be replete with terms such as "efficiency", "information asymmetry", "risk aversion", and "loss spreading". Likewise, if Andie's professor is The Philosopher, she is alert to any discussion of "rights", "duties", and similar normative terms.

Andie also recognizes that some of her peers are attempting to engage the professor's theory, and this is a second pool in which she does her fishing. Her challenge here is to separate those comments that advance her understanding of the theory from those that do not. Andie's rule of thumb in this regard is to ask, "Does this comment speak to my professor's point of view or past it?" For example, if the professor is a politician who believes that contract law is essentially an inequitable system that serves politically powerful mercantile interests, then comments utilizing the language of rights and duties—as determined by an unbiased arbiter—cannot speak to that professor in a meaningful way. This has less to do with the quality of the comment itself than with the fact that the professor rejects the fundamental assumption on which it is based: that matters of contract law can be determined in a manner that is not biased toward either plaintiff or defendant. Contributions that speak past her professor may be well presented and appealing to Andie. Nonetheless, she recognizes their limitations.

Returning to *Hadley* v. *Baxendale*, Andie recognizes from the outset that this case can be described from numerous perspectives. For example, The Economist might support the decision on the basis that it eliminates information asymmetry by encouraging customers who possess information about their particular needs to disclose that information to those carrying their goods. The Philosopher, meanwhile, might see the case as part of a larger system of contract law in which the rights of plaintiff and defendant are determined based on what can be objectively inferred from their agreement and irrespective of the external social or political consequences of any particular ruling. Doctor Doctrine, meanwhile, might question the extent to which the test of reasonably foreseeable damages as set forth in the decision can be applied in practice.

It is worth lingering on Doctor Doctrine for a moment because he poses a special problem for Andie. Because Doctor Doctrine has no particular vision of the law, the dominant strategy in his class is simply to know the cases. This strategy plays to Billie's strengths, and indeed, in Doctor Doctrine's class, the differences between Andie and Billie will be less prominent. Nonetheless, even in a class with Doctor Doctrine, Andie is attuned to the fact that some pieces of information are more important than others. Although Doctor Doctrine does not have a theory *per se*, he still has a pat way of summarizing a case or a body of cases, and Andie does her best to identify these pithy statements of law. Billie, in his mad scribbling, will undoubtedly include these pithy statements among his voluminous notes, but he will not be able to recognize them for the Big Bills that they are.

By figuring out her professor's theory of the law and learning how to "speak his language" Andie can tailor her note-taking to emphasize those arguments that are essential to further developing her understanding of her professor's theory.

When and How to Speak Up in Class

We have already seen that when Billie speaks up in class, he only responds to questions that have an obvious answer. Factual questions allow him to show that he has done the readings, but he shies away from questions to which he does not have immediate answers. In addition to the need to show himself to be intelligent and diligent, Billie may also have a desire to hear his own voice. Often, Billie will be heard chipping in some irrelevant comment or perhaps correcting the professor on some small detail.

Andie, in contrast, engages in the discussion of more challenging questions raised by the professor. Additionally, she asks questions of the professor that help her challenge and develop her understanding of the professor's theory. For example, if she has problems with the concept of foreseeability, she asks her professor what he thinks foreseeability means. The professor may then provide her with some examples (Andie might pose some examples of her own), and she may thereby find out that the professor admits that the concept is problematic. Alternatively, Andie's professor may talk about the concept as serving to allocate economic risks between the parties. "Unexpected risks," he might say, "must be borne by those best able to bear them because…" By asking questions in class, Andie, unlike Billie, learns what her professor thinks about the particular area of law she is studying and she clears up those specific details of the course that she finds confusing. Billie might be right in pointing out that the professor mixed up the authors of the majority and dissenting opinions in a particular case, but while he is proudly displaying the counterfeit penny he found, Andie is busy lining her pockets with real C-notes.

Once Andie has identified the sort of professor with whom she is dealing, she can ask questions to help solidify her understanding of the professor's approach. Doctor Doctrine, for example, will be primarily interested in the extent to which the rule in a particular case can be reconciled with other rules in a given area of law. Accordingly, when discussing *Hadley* v. *Baxendale* Andie might ask how the rule in the case would apply to a situation in which the plaintiff notified the defendant of his special circumstances *after* the agreement was made but *before* the defendant breached. Or, Andie might ask how this case fits with or conflicts with another case dealing with damages for breach of contract. Knowing that Doctor Doctrine will be less interested in engaging the case at the level of abstract principles, (his approach disavows the value of such considerations), she will avoid questions pitched at that level.

The Economist, by way of contrast, will be concerned with which economic principle is driving the ruling in *Hadley* v. *Baxendale*. Accordingly, Andie might ask the following questions. Is this case about encouraging plaintiff customers to divulge information about the losses they might incur to defendant carriers? Which party is the least cost avoider of this loss in the sense that it is better situated to anticipate it by virtue of its relative size and experience? Should it matter if the carrier in this case was better able to bear the loss by spreading it over a large customer base?

As the preceding narrative makes clear, there is no standard set of questions to ask in class. Rather, there is an overall approach. The questions Andie asks are dictated by the professor who is teaching the class and the extent to which she is familiar with his theory. In other words, Andie asks questions for strategic purposes, not simply to hear her own voice or impress her classmates and professor.

Of course, sometimes Andie finds herself without even a basic idea of what her professor's theory is. At such times, she may be sitting in a class thinking, "His reasoning is awfully slippery, and I have no idea what he's talking about." This is one instance in which Andie's having her own theory of the law begins to pay dividends. That theory helps her to formulate some understanding of the course and gives her a basis on which to begin teasing out her professor's understanding. For example, Andie may find her professor's view of contract law does not acknowledge the moral obligation to keep one's promises, an idea that she may see as being a fundamental theme underlying contract law. If she explains that her confusion comes from her acceptance of this idea, her professor will address her understanding and explain why his is better. He might say, for example, that the moral obligation to keep promises is irrelevant because what contract law really seeks to do is facilitate economic transactions. He will likely provide her with examples of how this is borne out in other areas of the case law and may even point to weaknesses in Andie's theory that she had not previously considered. The result of such transactions is that Andie is able to refine her own view of things while gaining a foothold into her professor's theory.

Andie knows that the classroom is not the only place to pursue such discussions. Recognizing that her professor is an excellent resource, Andie uses her time after class to ask him questions that help advance her understanding of the course material and, in particular, of his theory. When she sticks around after class and asks questions about those aspects of the course that she finds challenging, Andie finds out that her professor is happy to talk to her. Indeed, this is how she obtains some of her best insights into her professor's big-picture view. For while the professor's in-class discussion is usually constrained by the course requirements as set out in the syllabus, after class he is free to engage in a far-ranging discussion in which he will happily expound on his personal views.

Knowing When Not to Go to Class

Having spent a fair bit of time thinking about what to do when in class, it is worthwhile at this point to pose a question that is considered taboo by those who purport to take the study of law seriously: Should one even bother to attend class at all?

For Billie, this is a question that never comes up. For Charlie, it is one that is never far from his mind. Andie is the only one of our three protagonists who approaches the question in a systematic fashion. In answering it, she first of all recognizes that the course material has to get into her head somehow. That said, attending class is not the only alternative. Generally speaking, in a class where the professor merely summarizes cases, Andie is less likely to attend. Little can be gained from going to such a class. After all, Andie may be able to secure Billie's notes and, in any event, she will be sure to gain access to a good summary produced by a Billie from a previous year. With some professors, Andie can walk into a couple of classes with an old summary, and it is virtually a matter of following the bouncing ball with little in the way of questions or class participation. In addition to being rather useless, these classes are exceedingly dull. Under those circumstances, Andie knows that she is better off reviewing the summary and discussing it with her friends.

More commonly, the professor will be doing something beyond merely summarizing the cases, and in these circumstances Andie recognizes that attending class is an effective way of learning the material. The time commitment is relatively small, and the dividends are potentially quite large. It will be difficult for Andie to skip class and acquire the depth of understanding that she can develop there without a larger investment of time. On the other hand, Andie keeps in mind her reasons for attending class. She knows that to the extent that she is treating class attendance as a mere ritual, she is wasting her time. The classroom is not some sort of minimum-security prison facility and it should not be treated as such. If she is bored, she thinks about how she can make going to class engaging, whether by getting to class on time, doing her reading in advance, talking to her friends or the professor about the material, or getting involved in class discussion.

Having given it an honest try, if Andie still finds herself bored and annoyed she will not bother going to class. There is no point in being like Charlie in the classroom since doing so will leave her feeling discouraged and too tired to make up for what she missed in class. By not going, she has more time to do what she enjoys doing, and she is no worse off than if she sat in the physical space, tuned out what was going on around her and read a magazine in the back row while waiting for the time to pass. Charlie's approach to classroom learning is analogous to pushing against a brick wall. He expends a great deal of effort but accomplishes nothing.

Take It *to the* BANK:
Big Bills for CLASS ATTENDANCE

$ Pay special attention to class discussion — this is where the biggest insights lie.
$ Be sure to ask your professor questions directed at discerning his or her preferred theory, both in and outside of class.
$ Pay attention in class or don't go at all.
$ Make a choice and stick with it. Either attend class or don't.

In any event, whether Andie chooses to attend class or not, she will as always be systematic in her conduct. That is, if for reasons just outlined she decides that class attendance is unnecessary, she will remain faithful to this decision. The need Charlie feels to alleviate his sense of guilt by attending class sporadically is one that Andie will consciously resist. She knows, after all, that trying to pick up the thread of classroom discussion after two weeks of truancy is both hopeless and pointless: again, her time is better spent elsewhere. Thus, Andie's decision to not attend class — for all intents and purposes — is a once and for all decision.

When Andie does decide to skip class, she realistically takes stock of what she is missing. Where the professor merely summarizes the cases, she is not missing anything that she cannot pick up from a summary. Often, though, she may have to think a bit harder to make up for missed class time through some other method of learning that she finds more palatable. Ultimately, Andie knows that the important thing is for her to formulate an understanding of the law in her own head. Nobody cares whether she does that by talking to friends, borrowing their notes, or bouncing ideas off others who have been to class.

Reading Cases

On her first day Andie runs into Billie (Class of '98). "Going to get books?" he asks, "Hope you brought a pickup!" Billie's admonishment is indicative of the posturing regarding the inordinate amount of reading first-year law students are expected to do. Advice on this point often tends toward the mythic and fantastic rather than the realistic. Admittedly, there is a great deal of reading to be done in first year—perhaps more than in any other year—and at times anybody can feel overwhelmed. Andie's strategy, in the face of this, is to minimize—ideally to eliminate—those occasions on which she feels overworked, by keeping in mind her overarching goal: to achieve academic success with a minimum of pain.

Billie, in comparison, embraces the pain, spending countless hours in the library and reading every word that has been assigned. He researches related but unassigned cases; he even combs the material referenced in the

> "I read so much in first year that I lost my 20/20 vision!"

footnotes. Billie's eyes pass over a great deal of verbiage, and in the process, he will undoubtedly fill his piggybank one penny at a time. But at what cost? The mere sight of Billie inspires anxiety in his classmates and because they are Billies too, law school becomes an upward spiral of ever-mounting anxiety leading to ever-increasing effort.

Underlying Billie's behaviour is the assumption that there is some necessary connection between pain and gain and that without hours spent in lonely and monastic contemplation, there can be no enlightenment. The acceptance of this line of reasoning is also exemplified in Charlie's behaviour. At first, this manifests itself in Charlie's efforts to emulate Billie. Because he thinks that he has to be like Billie in order to succeed, he lazily goes through Billie's rituals. He spends time in the library, but he wastes most of it, desperately seeking distractions with the result that he accomplishes little and does not enjoy himself either. When he reads, eyes fluttering with boredom and exhaustion, he retains little.

Charlie may find himself sitting in a library having read four pages in the last two hours and feeling extremely fatigued. This is part of the vicious cycle. Eventually, Charlie may realize the pointlessness of staring at words on a page, leading him to break out of this cycle and cease reading altogether. Charlie's strategy would be fantastic if it was not for the fact that he has to write exams on this material. Charlie has purchased his free time on credit and at some point he will have to pay for it with interest. Not only will Charlie have to suffer increased anxiety as exam time rolls around, but his grades will also suffer.

Andie, in contrast, thinks about why she is supposed to read cases rather than neurotically memorizing every word of assigned reading. Her casebooks, voluminous as they are, are not there for her to memorize. It is true that memorizing all the material might work, but thinking that reading, reviewing, and memorizing every word is the only way to succeed seems a lot like thinking that running through a brick wall is the only way to get to the other side. The fact is that — the mythology of legal education notwithstanding — there are not that many brick walls through which one needs to run in law school. Rather, there are plenty of doors, shortcuts, and footholds to help one get where one wants to go.

Let's be honest — reading cases can be painful and time-consuming. The material is often extremely detailed, long-winded, and dry. It is possible to spend a number of hours reading an eighty-page case and learn *absolutely nothing*. One can easily get bogged down in the details of the case, especially when they appear to be driving the decision. To make matters even worse, cases are assigned in groups, and the assigned cases often seem to stand for entirely contradictory propositions. Thus, reading can be confusing as well as tedious.

Paradoxically, though the cases themselves are extraordinarily detail oriented and lengthy, Andie knows that the ultimate task is to synthesize that material into something short, sweet, and pithy. What separates Andie from her less evolved classmates is that she recognizes that she need not do all her reading to accomplish this. Rather, the casebook is one of many tools available to develop an understanding of the law. For Andie, reading cases is not some masochistic ritual to be observed with unwavering devotion; it is part of a larger process of learning, to be done on an as-needed basis.

Like the classroom strategy outlined earlier, Andie's approach to reading cases looks like Billie's at first, but evolves into something very different. Andie recognizes that she is embarking on something new, and, therefore, she expects to have to work at things a bit harder initially. Unlike Charlie, however, Andie does not despair. She realizes that after spending a month or two reading cases, she will have picked up most of the Big Bills to be gained from doing so and will not need to worry about whether she can compete with Billie's eight months of hard labour. Unlike Billie and Charlie, Andie thinks strategically about her work from day one such that she will find at least some of the shortcuts that are available to her. Why must this be so, one might ask? Because Andie, unlike Billie and Charlie who deny the existence of shortcuts, believes in their existence and is actively looking for them. It should come as no surprise that she who seeks shall find.

Andie, then, spends the first weeks (perhaps even months) of law school learning the skill of reading cases. It is not too stressful an experience since she recognizes that she is learning something from the exercise. At any rate, the exam is not in September, and indeed, to be challenged and perhaps even confused at times is part of what it is to learn. This mindset makes it more likely that Andie will find her reading interesting rather than unpleasant. The goal of Andie's reading is not to memorize the details of the case — the exam will not test such details — but rather, to acquire a comfort level with reading cases. Having acquired this level of familiarity, Andie soon realizes that there is no magic in learning *how* to read cases. There is, however, some skill required in knowing *what* and *when* to read. This means that Andie begins trying out some of the shortcuts that are available to her in order to see which ones work best. As Andie begins to find these shortcuts, Billie continues to stress over every detail, big or small. Charlie, meanwhile, has long since given up.

So what are these shortcuts? For starters, Andie approaches her readings by thinking about why a case has been assigned. The course syllabus and the table of contents in her casebook are helpful in this regard. The heading under which a particular case is discussed helps orient her as to what she should focus on. This seems obvious, but it is amazing how many people overlook this.

Furthermore, Andie realizes that not all cases are of equal importance. Some cases are there merely for historical background or context. Moreover, the length of these less meaningful decisions is often disproportionate to their value. Thus, there is no need to spend a great deal of time examining them as long as Andie has a handle on the leading cases.

How, one might ask, does Andie determine what these leading cases are? If Andie does her reading before class, how will she be able to identify and weed out less important cases in advance? One obvious answer is that she may in fact not read cases before class. Instead, she may spend a few moments reading a headnote or somebody else's summary to orient herself for class discussion, leaving reading of the actual case, if needed, to a later time. Because of this, Andie will have the benefit of the professor's exegesis in class to help her determine what the leading cases are. Moreover, Andie can always turn to another resource, perhaps a textbook or the summary itself, for an indication of which are the leading cases. Finally, as we suggested in the last chapter, Andie's use of unifying concepts helps her systematize class material in such a way as to bring to light the relative significance of details.

Andie can remain confident that her strategy entails no real risk because she always keeps in mind her ultimate goal, which is to distill each case into a pithy sentence or two. Given this goal, Andie need not spend hours reading an eighty-page decision. Although it is true that Andie may spend time reading cases in some detail, she will focus on leading cases and in particular on key passages. Although she does not have Billie's religious fervour for doing readings, Andie often finds that by the time the exam rolls around, she has "read" a good number of the cases assigned in her class. This is so, even though she has read very few cases in advance of class and may not have read the full text of any one judgment.

Andie's approach is not only more efficient than Billie's, it also acknowledges the availability of other, potentially more valuable, resources than the cases themselves. There are only so many hours in the day, and even Billie has his breaking point. Recognizing this, Andie employs substitutes for case reading that provide her with a better understanding of the course. To begin with, there is somebody else's summary. This is a good resource for the nuts and bolts of the cases. As well, to the extent that Andie has friends who are Billies, she may ask to borrow their class notes. Andie will not stop there, however.

Unlike Billie, who is hunkered down in the library climbing Mount Casebook, Andie will have plenty of free time on her hands. Some of this free time will be spent seeking out other resources such as textbooks and articles written by her professor. Textbooks are very helpful to Andie in learning a course, particularly those aspects which she finds confusing or challenging. By spending time studying only cases, it is very easy for Billie to "lose the forest for the trees." The difficulty for Billie is trying to synthesize several hundred pages of material into some sort of larger understanding. Billie may spend the afternoon reading three or four conflicting cases — each thirty or more pages long — and come away confused. Moreover, Billie may have deluded himself into thinking that he has achieved an understanding simply because he has passed his eyes over a mountain of assigned pages. The danger in this is that he does not even realize what he is missing. A textbook would summarize those very same cases for him in a concise and user-friendly way. Andie, by reading the textbook, will often find that she has spent less time and has a better grasp of the material than Billie, who spent hours slugging it out with the casebook. Accordingly, Andie will always ask her professor for the name of a good textbook on the subject.

Papers written by Andie's professor and those academics who share his theory are also excellent resources. Admittedly, there will be too much of this material for her to read it all, but she can ask her professor to direct her to some especially helpful samples. By using these sorts of papers to supplement textbooks, Andie finds that she can often succeed in a law school class doing surprisingly little in the way of assigned readings.

The purpose of the foregoing is not to discourage the reading of cases. Rather, it is to suggest that cases are simply one resource among many. The extent to which Andie draws from any one of these as opposed to another depends on a variety of factors: most notably, time. The important thing is that Andie asks herself what she is getting out of reading cases, rather than simply reading that which is assigned to the exclusion of all else.

Take It to the BANK: Big Bills for READING CASES

$ There is no need to memorize cases. Use your casebook as one of many available tools.

$ All cases are not equal. Focus on figuring out what the leading cases are and direct your energies toward these.

$ Never underestimate the value of secondary sources, especially a text-book or artcles written by your professor.

Studying outside of CLASS

Consider the following. Charlie, enjoying a night on the town at the local pub, spots Andie having a beer with some friends. "Hey, Andie, what are you up to?" Charlie asks. "Oh, we're just studying contracts," she says. "Yeah, right, me too," he responds with a wink, and walks off to the bar. Charlie simply cannot believe that Andie could be doing anything productive at the pub. After all, studying is done in painful solitude or in some dull seminar room. Well, isn't it?

One of the most intellectually rewarding and enjoyable aspects of law school is the study group. Ideally, the study group is where one's essential understanding of the law crystallizes, where the big picture "all comes together." It is an attractive vision—ambitious and thoughtful peers coming together and grappling with grand ideas. In the end, they achieve some sort of wisdom, a certain understanding, and the result, of course, is academic success. In practice, this vision is difficult to realize. For Billie himself often joins a study group for reasons quite independent of this. Thus the kind of study group that typically forms—full of Billies (and the occasional Charlie hanger-on)—is liable to render the experience somewhat dull and tedious.

Moreover, study groups can be somewhat elitist. Billie's first instinct, after all, is to "go it alone"—studying late into the night by himself and scorning the contributions of others. For him, law school is a zero-sum game in which everyone competes. Given this, cooperation makes sense only if one can form an alliance among the best students. Billie believes that he can ensure his own success only by combining his own mental energies with those of some predetermined group of *über*-students.

This approach to the study group is doomed almost from the outset. As has already been discussed, the cooperation that is essential to the study group is unlikely to arise where one recognizes fellow group members as competitors at the end of the day. The members of such a group, even if they are truly "the best," are likely to withhold information from each other and fail to realize their very reason for coming together. Indeed, it is likely that this group will degenerate into a collection of individuals that spend their days poring over material they may or may not enjoy with people they may or may not like. This is a far cry from the noble fellowship that a study group is supposed to be.

Billie's problem is that he makes what is predominantly a social decision—the choice of who to study with—based on instrumental considerations. In fairness to him, however, Billie cannot possibly make his decision based on the correct criteria: for he starts looking to form a group too early. Being "all business," Billie begins looking for a study group within the first few weeks of school, or at any rate certainly no later than when the first graded piece of work comes back, since that will give him the necessary information about who to seek out.

Charlie, meanwhile, suffers from a similar problem. Having at first disdained the very idea of a study group on the basis that it could offer only more of the same kind of pain that he seeks to avoid, Charlie will eventually, under pressure from impending exams, be forced to seek out the assistance of others. He, like Billie, will be instrumentalist in his choice and indeed he will likely attempt to hook up with a group of Billies. This makes sense since Billie's disciplined and serious demeanour gives him the superficial appearance of the ideal law student. In a pinch, this sort of person will have a powerful magnetism for a panicky Charlie. Charlie might privately think of Billie as a humourless geek, but the possibility of sponging off an interactive encyclopedia might cause him to tolerate the company of a person with whom he otherwise would not dream of spending time. Charlie naively assumes that as long as he can swing an invite to the party, a room full of Billies will happily share their best thoughts and ideas with him. He will not even question whether they are holding back from each other.

Andie is unlike Charlie and Billie in that she views collaborating with others not as a necessary evil to be endured for instrumental reasons but as potentially the most rewarding aspect of her legal education. The rewards can be measured both objectively, in terms of academic success, and subjectively, in terms of the enjoyment and understanding that comes from sharing interesting conversations with one's friends. Moreover, these are not discrete benefits, but benefits that are mutually reinforcing. The more one enjoys one's time discussing course material, the more one's understanding will increase, and this in turn will increase the enthusiasm with which one approaches further conversation.

In view of this, the pub (or some similar location) is where Andie does much of her best work. It is true that at some point she will have to retreat to a quiet place alone to review things, and it is equally true that at some point (usually fairly close to the exam) she will have to turn up the intensity and do a good deal of serious studying in a quiet place that is free from distraction (although not in solitude). But for the overwhelming majority of the semester (and as we will see in chapter 4, even when she is studying for exams), Andie studies in a relatively comfortable environment with people whose company she enjoys.

Andie, recognizing the pitfalls of joining a study group of strangers, is in no hurry to join one. Rather, she takes her time and gets used to her new surroundings. Eventually, she makes some new friends, and at that point, she is in a position to begin studying with others in a manner that is infinitely more enjoyable and academically rewarding than the neurosis-charged business meetings that her colleagues schedule.

Although it is true that Andie's study group may not get off the ground spontaneously, it is also true that people come to law school because they have something more than a marginal interest in the subject matter. At some point, Andie finds that she is going for lunch or a beer with a couple of friends. When she turns the conversation to something that was talked about in class, her friends have some of their own ideas and opinions about the cases and their professor's approach. This sort of conversation arises quite naturally, but this is no less a study group than Billie's. Indeed, as has already been suggested, it is much more.

Andie knows that one of the great things about law school is that she and her friends have a ton of free time. As a result of this, there is no need to introduce the tediousness of schedules, meetings at the library, and the other suits and trappings of the business world that make study group an empty experience for Billie and utter hell for Charlie. Study group is simply what Andie does for part of the time when she is hanging out with her friends, at lunch, at the bar, or at the coffee shop.

Because Andie views studying as something that happens when hanging out with her friends, it does not happen at some pre-ordained time or with some predetermined frequency. It happens pretty much every day. Talking with her friends about a particular case or idea is studying. The fact that she is not holed up in the library and bored out of her mind or meeting in some sterile seminar room does not make it any less so. There is nothing "unstudious" about learning the law by hanging out with friends and chatting about ideas over a beer or two.

If Andie's study group is different from Billie's in form, it is even more different in substance. Billie's study group resembles what he does in class and while studying on his own. Thus, he and his group pore over and review the assigned cases in excruciating detail. After all, if the way to learn cases is through memorization, then study group is merely an opportunity to review and memorize in the company of others. Andie, meanwhile, uses her conversations with her friends to refine her big-picture view of the course. Her study group is where she synthesizes the cases into the big picture that will enable her to deal with whatever new set of facts is thrown at her on the exam. While Billie and his gang go over fact, issue, decision, and reasons for each case, Andie and her friends think about what all this means.

For example, consider the following discussion in which Andie and two of her friends attempt to synthesize *Hadley* v. *Baxendale* into a larger theoretical framework. For the purposes of this discussion, assume that the class is being taught by The Philosopher.

Andie: I'm having a problem figuring out what *Hadley* v. *Baxendale* is all about.

Ashleigh: What's the problem?

Andie: Well, I know the case stands for the idea that if a party breaches a contract, he is only liable for consequential loss if the loss was reasonably foreseeable. And then there's this two-part test, which says that a reasonably foreseeable loss is one that was either ordinarily foreseeable or specifically communicated. But what does this actually mean? Put differently, how can one distinguish between an ordinarily foreseeable loss and one that has been specifically communicated?

Allie: I think what this case means is that in order to be reasonably foreseeable, the loss that actually happened has to be the sort of loss that every plaintiff would incur. Otherwise, there has to be some specific statement to get the defendant on the hook.

Andie: So let's say you're a jockey and you've signed up for the Belmont Stakes. I'm selling you a horse. I deliver the horse half a day late, and as a result you lose the opportunity to compete. You can somehow prove that you would have won if I had delivered on time (in fact, you can even prove that this was knowable in advance of the race itself). You suffered huge financial losses as a result of my failure to deliver on time. Can you recover?

Allie: Did you tell me anything about the race, and how you could guarantee a win?

Andie: No.

Allie: Then I've got to say that you're out of luck. It seems to me that the ordinary person wouldn't suffer that sort of loss simply because the horse was delivered half a day late. You contracted for a horse, and you got a horse. It happened to be half a day late, but how was I supposed to know what that would cost you?

Ashleigh: Fair enough, Allie, but what if we change the facts a bit? Let's say that you run a well-known stud farm and have been selling horses to Andie for years. In fact, you sold her the winning horse for the last Belmont as well as the other two Triple Crown races this year (again, in all these cases, Andie was able to prove in advance of the race itself that she would win). Now can you say her loss wasn't reasonably foreseeable?

Allie: Hmmm. My gut reaction says yes. I mean, I must have known that it would cost her a ton of money if I was late, but still, we contracted for the delivery of a horse. She didn't really tell me anything specific about her circumstances. I just happened to figure them out on my own, so I'm not sure how to resolve this given the test.

Ashleigh: Well, we could say that this is an ordinary loss. Andie did not contract the delivery of just any old horse. She contracted for a horse guaranteed to win the Belmont, to be delivered the day of the race. In that case, her financial loss seems pretty ordinary.

Allie: I see your point, but it seems odd that her special circumstances somehow change what is an ordinary loss. I thought that the question we were asking was whether or not this sort of loss would arise in all circumstances, so why are we taking account of her individual circumstances when asking that question? Doesn't that obliterate the distinction between the two branches of the test?

Andie: That's what I was wondering. It seems to me that the first part of the test has something to do with a hypothetical plaintiff. In other words, we ask in the abstract whether or not all plaintiffs would suffer this loss. If the answer here is no, then we move to the second branch of the test and ask about this particular plaintiff. Has she done anything to make the loss ordinarily foreseeable? If not, she's out of luck.

Allie: Right, but then we have Ashleigh's characterization problem. Whether this is ordinary depends on how we describe the horse that is the subject matter of the contract. Is it just any old horse we're talking about, or is it a horse that is guaranteed to win the Belmont Stakes?

Ashleigh: I'm wondering if there's a way out of this problem. I mean, what is the larger principle here?

Allie: When I asked myself that question, I thought this might have something to do with the equality of the plaintiff and defendant.

Ashleigh: How so?

Allie: Well, let's remember what a remedy for breach of contract does. It places the parties in the position they would have been in had the contract been performed. In other words, it says to the defendant, if you breach, we're going to make you pay damages that represent the amount of money the plaintiff lost as a reasonably foreseeable consequence of your breach. This respects the equality of the parties since what the plaintiff gets is entirely determined by the parties' mutual agreement.

Andie: Exactly. So, when we speak about reasonably foreseeable consequences, we are simply asking what the parties intended. Did they see this loss as being the sort of loss that would arise from the defendant's breach?

Ashleigh: So let me get this straight. We see this case as saying that, at a minimum, the equality of the parties requires the defendant to be liable for the sort of loss that any plaintiff would suffer. That's what the ordinary loss part is about. The specific communication part of the test says that if the plaintiff wants the defendant to be liable for something particular to her, she can't impose these subjective preferences on the defendant.

Andie: Right. The defendant is not bound by the plaintiff's preferences unless she makes those preferences known, in which case, they are rendered objective as between the parties.

Allie: That makes sense. Since the equality of the parties requires us to interpret their mutual intention from an objective perspective — one that ignores the individual preferences of each of them — we should expect this case to work within the same analytical framework.

Ashleigh: So, if we've got the general principle, what work is this test doing for us?

Andie: I think it gives us a specific instance of the general principle. We know that consequential loss is different, and we now have a more refined language to sort out recoverable losses from unrecoverable losses. Determining which branch of the test a given loss falls under may be difficult in some circumstances, but I'm not sure that serves as a criticism of the test.

Ashleigh: Right. But I find this test a bit slippery in practice.

Andie: Fair enough, but we know that tests don't apply themselves. We understand the significance of reasonable foreseeability, and we have some idea of what this means in practice.

Ashleigh: And the problem of characterizing something as ordinarily foreseeable as opposed to specifically communicated?

Andie: I'm not sure if that matters as much. If we speak in terms of the general category of reasonable foreseeability and ask what appears to be the objective manifestation of the parties' intentions, we get the answer we need. The sub-categories embodied in the test can do some work, but it looks like there are going to be characterization problems there.

Allie: That makes sense to me.

Ashleigh: I think we've got it then. Still, next time I get a chance, I'm going to ask The Philosopher if he thinks we're on the right track here.

Notice that in the preceding discussion, Andie and her friends spent little time discussing the nuts and bolts of the case. Rather, they had a conversation in order to resolve a difficulty that one of them was having with an aspect of the course. In addressing this difficulty, they attempted to view the case from their professor's own preferred theoretical perspective. As they were in The Philosopher's class, they sought guidance from the language of philosophy. They arrived at a resolution that appeared to accord with The Philosopher's larger theory. Finally, they recognized that there was an opportunity to follow up with The Philosopher in order to ensure that they had arrived at the correct understanding.

Moreover, Andie and her friends enjoyed engaging in this conversation because it was pitched at a more interesting level than the sort of studying that is generally done in a study group comprised of strangers. Given that the discussion arose in the context of casual conversation, it was likely surrounded by less erudite but equally amusing dialogue, much of which may have been unprintable. By studying in this manner throughout the semester, Andie and her friends manage to refine their understanding of the course material in a manner that is both enjoyable and academically stimulating.

three

PREPARING
for Exams

HINK back to the basketball analogy in the last chapter. We saw how our characters go about developing their overall basketball skills. Suppose now that it is a couple of weeks before tryouts. How do you think each of our three characters prepares? Who do you think has the most fun getting ready for the "basketball exam"? Who, moreover, has the best chance of doing well at the tryout and making the team?

Billie, not surprisingly, changes nothing in the face of the impending tryout, except of course to do more of the same thing he has done all along. Instead of 100 laps around the court and 200 free throws, he does 200 laps and shoots 400 free throws. Instead of eight sets of calf raises, he does sixteen sets. Make no mistake: all this will leave Billie in an enviable state of physical fitness. His body fat will be 5 percent, and his heart rate at rest can be expected to be in the mid-50s. Billie may be ready to run a marathon, but unfortunately it's a basketball tryout he will be confronted with. No doubt he has a 42-inch vertical and can shoot free throws with 90 percent accuracy, but everything changes in a game situation. Shooting free throws in an empty gym is not at all like putting up a 12-foot jumper with someone's hand in your face and under the watchful scrutiny of a critical coach. Moreover, Billie is ill equipped to adapt to the ebb and flow of the game itself, to deal with its situational dynamics. Indeed, every situation that arises on the court is bound to seem entirely new and unfamiliar to him.

Charlie also approaches the upcoming tryout true to form. Seeing Billie step up the intensity of his own workouts, Charlie decides he had better give the gym another shot. Unfortunately, the experience reminds him of why he gave up going to the gym months ago. He spends one day lifting weights but awakens the next morning stiff and sore. Rather than continue to submit to the agony, he reassures himself that strength and flexibility won't make much difference come tryout day. In fact, he has heard from a veteran member of the team that on tryout day it's all a question of whether or not you get lucky and make your shots. So Charlie fritters his time away playing video games and sleeping late. The night before the big tryout, in a fit of anxiety, Charlie realizes that he is woefully unprepared. He stays up late into the night trying to make up for lost time by doing pushups and calf raises and shooting free throws until he gets thrown out of the gym. Fearing that this still isn't enough, Charlie watches the last half of the Lakers–Clippers game on TV. Just before going to bed that night he realizes that he may need high-tops and calls up Bobbie to see if he can borrow a pair. After a couple of hours of fitful sleep he wakes in time (or so he thinks) to make a failed attempt at braiding his hair into cornrows. Breakfast gets cut short because he has to swing by Bobbie's place to pick up the high-tops. Unfortunately, this takes more time than he anticipated, and he shows up at the tryout just late enough for the coach to make a mental note of his tardiness. On top of his lateness, general fatigue from lack of sleep, a skipped breakfast, and the stiffness and soreness from the hardest workout since the night before last year's tryout leave Charlie with little prospect of making the team. Luckily, the inevitable disappointment will not last long: by tomorrow Charlie will already have convinced himself that basketball is a ridiculous pursuit that he never really cared about anyway.

Unlike her two counterparts, Andie understands that success on tryout day will not strictly depend on her level of fitness, but also on her ability to scrimmage. As we mentioned in the last chapter, this includes, among other things, her ability to see the overall development of the play, her awareness of which plays will work in different situations, and in general her "understanding" of the game. She continues to develop all these skills by playing basketball with a group of friends for several hours a day leading up to tryouts. Consequently, when tryout day arrives, Andie is prepared. By this we do not mean physically prepared (though certainly her technical abilities and level of fitness have improved as a result of the hours she has spent scrimmaging); we mean *totally* prepared. No matter what situation arises in the scrimmage, Andie has seen some variant of it. She has put up countless jumpers with a hand in her face. She recognizes a pick and roll and knows how to defend it. In short, she understands the game itself *and* her coach's preferred system of play. Given this, it is not surprising that Andie makes the starting lineup while Billie rides the pine and Charlie watches from the stands, telling everyone within earshot that he could have made the team if not for the raw deal he got from the coach.

As with preparation for a basketball tryout, so with preparation for law school exams. Never is Billie more Billie than in the month before his first exam. He practically lives in the library, focusing his will intensely on the attainment of one simple goal: amassing an impressive catalogue of legal trivia. To give his intensity a tangible manifestation he has not shaved in weeks: after all, everyone should have a "playoff beard." Billie knows that as exams draw closer his life will grow increasingly difficult and lonely, but in his eyes, that's just the proof of how well he will do. Indeed, Billie's mantra when it comes to exam preparation is reflective of a common misconception capitalized on in the marketing campaign of a certain cough syrup manufacturer: if it didn't taste bad, it probably wouldn't work. Of course, the natural response is that if it doesn't work, an even worse taste will be left in one's mouth, and there are all sorts of reasons why it might not work.

Nor is Charlie's approach likely to meet with much greater success. Where Billie sees the period leading up to exams as the time in which one's will becomes tempered through suffering, Charlie dreads it as the time when his enjoyment of life will suffer through temperance. Of course, having no stomach for this kind of suffering, Charlie soon falls off the wagon. Fearing the sting of failed effort, Charlie soon rejects the Billie ethos entirely by eschewing Billie's most sacred value—exam success.

Unfortunately for Charlie, his latent Billieness often resurfaces in the day or two prior to the exam. He typically has a sudden realization that he cannot, on pain of shattering his own self-image, completely leave his exam results to chance. Driven by guilt, he therefore makes a last-ditch attempt to learn the material. Charlie's desperate efforts may save him from complete failure, but they give the lie to his principles. After all, if grade anxiety was beneath him two weeks before the exam, why should it suddenly become a legitimate concern ten or twelve days later?

Evidently, then, we have little to learn from Charlie — or, for that matter, Billie — when it comes to exam preparation. Indeed, we have already seen the weaknesses in their respective approaches to law school in other contexts. It is to be expected that those weaknesses will simply become amplified as their approaches become intensified in the lead-up to exams.

Indeed, of our three stars, Andie is the only one who adapts her law school strategy to take account of the fact that scrimmaging during the semester is very different from scrimmaging in preparation for the exam. With this in mind, Andie hones her skills to ensure that she is able to adapt to any potential "game" situation. The key to doing so lies in Andie's ability to correctly identify the nature of the "game" she is playing.

So what does this game require? What is the law exam equivalent of being able to read the play as it develops or hit a 12-footer with a hand in your face? To begin with, just as reading the play in basketball requires an understanding of the system the coach wants implemented, so too being able to "read the play" in an exam requires an understanding of your professor's theory of the course. This is by now a familiar theme. Although Andie has been trying to figure out her professor's theory all year, her efforts in this regard become more focused in the period immediately preceding exams. Andie's focus is on the various implications of her professor's preferred theory, not in the abstract, but in connection with all the bits of legal data or trivia that comprise the substance of a course.

The process of mastering important facts and understanding the nuances of key cases can be likened to running laps or doing calf raises. It's a long and uncomfortable process that carries a high cost, but is nonetheless indispensable to one's overall exam fitness. Billie loves running laps. Charlie fears and loathes the pain and drudgery it entails. Andie, to be sure, is not very keen on this sort of training either, but rather than surrender its benefits she finds more effective and palatable ways to run her laps.

Collaborative Studying

First and foremost, this means running in a pack. Most of Andie's study techniques involve collaborative learning. As the last chapter suggested, Andie will have established her "study group" by now. When the end of the semester nears, her study group begins making the transition to exam-preparation mode. That transition is made natural by the fact that Andie has been hanging out and discussing legal issues with her friends throughout the semester. In a sense, she has therefore been "studying" all along. It is now just a question of injecting more structure and focus into these lunchtime discussions. The necessary structure and focus is provided by various techniques that the study group begins to implement as part of its exam preparation. Examples of these techniques include The Page Flip, Tiger Spotting, Story Telling, The Association Game, composing a High Level Summary, and doing practice exams.

Study Techniques

The Page Flip

The Page Flip is where Andie's exam preparation is likely to start. This is exactly what it sounds like: it consists of going through a course summary page by page. In the last chapter, we indicated the importance of having a prior year's summary. It is worth mentioning at this point that Andie and her friends should all work from the same summary throughout the semester. The rationale for this is clear: namely, so that when exam preparation begins, all members of the group can be "on the same page" as it were.

In all probability Andie and her group will do several Page Flips through their summary. The first one will involve going through everything in close detail. Of course, on subsequent Page Flips the group can begin to ignore relatively less important parts of the summary, but initially they will pay careful attention to anything that has not been explicitly identified by the professor as irrelevant for exam purposes. As they do their Page Flip, Andie and her friends develop their understanding of the course by asking each other questions about the material. They get into (sometimes heated) discussions.

They argue over why they agree or do not agree with the outcome of a case. If something about a case troubles Andie but she is not quite sure why, she does her best to articulate her concern and allows the group to decide whether it is serious and, if so, what can be done about it.

Benefits of The Page Flip

As one can see, The Page Flip is, through and through, an interactive studying experience. Because of this, it offers special benefits as a method of learning the nuts and bolts of the course. Through it, the tedium involved in getting intimately familiar with the details of the course material, which we have likened to running laps, is converted into an agreeable social endeavour.

Moreover, The Page Flip offers Andie the benefit of her friends' insights and perspectives on various issues raised by the material. This allows Andie to avoid a pitfall to which Billie often falls prey: a false sense of security. Billie feels secure when he's working hard. He will go to sleep feeling confident if he worked for ten hours that day. His mistake is that he equates how many hours he spends working with how prepared he is for an exam. Andie realizes that sitting in some lonely corner of the library is not only an excruciatingly painful way to learn, it is also an ineffective habit that will fail to alert her to the weaknesses in her understanding. Things that appear to make sense to us on a first—and all too often superficial—reading can often be exposed as problematic by our peers. It is only when we ask others questions about the material, and have questions asked of us, that we become able to assess the strength of our understanding. This is what studying in a group—and in particular The Page Flip—allows for.

Of course, these benefits are nothing new to Andie: she has already been enjoying them as a result of what she and her friends have been doing in study group all semester long. There is, however, one difference: up until now, Andie and her friends have mainly discussed random and seemingly disconnected cases that they found especially interesting or problematic from the perspective of their professor's preferred theory of the course. This has been helpful in establishing the theoretical framework within which The Page Flip is conducted. Now, however, the task is to systematically discuss each and every case in the context of that theory. The result is that the entire body of case law they are responsible for learning gets slotted together, like pieces in a theoretical puzzle, and problems which would otherwise have been overlooked are addressed and hopefully resolved. Thus, whereas past discussions have been kept at a higher level of generality, giving Andie a view of the overall picture of an area of law, The Page Flip descends into the nuances of the course material, giving Andie an awareness of how the various pieces of legal trivia fit together to form that picture. That is why The Page Flip is a suitable method for Andie to "run her laps," as it were, getting herself fit to write the exam.

Tiger Spotting

Still, the analogy to running laps is somewhat imperfect (as analogies are wont to be). The benefits to be obtained from the Page Flip extend beyond mere "fitness," or mastery of the details of the course material. Through it, Andie is also able to develop her ability to "read the play," or anticipate the kinds of moves her professor will make on an exam. This skill is partially acquired through a related technique — Tiger Spotting.

Suppose one was asked to describe the essential features of a tiger. One might reply with a list that included some or all of the following: large feline, four legs, a tail, whiskers, sharp teeth, claws, and, of course, stripes. But what if one encountered a big cat with all these characteristics except for a tail. Would that still be a tiger? Probably. Well, what if it was a small cat? What if it only had three legs? What if it had no teeth or claws? The answer to whether one would still have a tiger would, in all these cases, involve considerable judgment, but at some point — perhaps when our animal no longer had stripes, or was not even a feline — we should be prepared to admit that we no longer had a tiger. The point is, we all think we know a tiger when we see one, but it can be a difficult call to make at the margins. The best we can do is to say that tigers have a certain cluster of features and the more of these features we can identify in the beast in front of us, the more likely it is that we have a tiger.

An essential task that confronts one in writing a law school exam can be likened to Tiger Spotting. Few things on a law school exam are cut and dried. Instead, law exams require us to apply legal rules to fact patterns that may or may not match the sets of facts that gave rise to those rules in the first place. Just as it is often difficult to apply the linguistic rule "tiger" to a creature that doesn't quite have the complete cluster of features, so it is difficult to apply legal rules to facts that do not quite match those we find in the cases themselves. Indeed, professors quite consciously go to great lengths on exams to devise factual "creatures" that are difficult to classify. As a result, in preparing for exams, it is at least as important to be attuned to ambiguity as it is to memorize hard and fast legal principles. Much of what one is asked to do on an exam involves reasoned characterization of an ambiguous set of facts. One must identify the beast as either a tiger or as something else and one must provide justifications for one's conclusions in this regard. Knowing this, Andie and her study group incorporate Tiger Spotting into their exam preparation.

In other words, they Tiger Spot while doing their Page Flips. This involves isolating certain facts in their discussion of the cases and asking what the significance of those facts is and how the Court's decision might have been different if those facts were slightly changed. Thus, they talk about things like what it would mean if the beast confronting them had spots instead of stripes. The way to prepare to spot tigers on an exam is to play with the sorts of features, or facts, that go into making up the beast.

Tiger Spotting: A Case Study

To get a better idea of exactly what is involved in Tiger Spotting, let's eavesdrop on Andie and her friends as they discuss contract law. They are in the midst of their Page Flip. The topic of the day is (unsurprisingly) *Hadley* v. *Baxendale*.

Andie: Okay, someone tell me what this case is about and why it matters.

Allie: This case stands for the principle that the defendant is only responsible for losses that are reasonably foreseeable consequences of his breach of contract. Losses arising from a breach will be considered reasonably foreseeable if they are either ordinarily foreseeable in the circumstances or specifically communicated at the time of formation.

Ashleigh: What do you think would have happened if the mill owner told the carrier that it was extremely crucial that the shaft be delivered on time but didn't tell the carrier that he would suffer severe financial loss if it was delivered late? Should the carrier be liable for the owner's extraordinary loss if the shaft is then delivered late?

Andie: If on hearing this it became reasonably foreseeable that the owner would suffer financial loss if the product was delivered late, then he should be able to recover from the carrier. You could argue that the only reason that a factory owner would insist on prompt delivery is that the shaft was necessary to the operation of his factory and thus the word "crucial" would make economic loss reasonably foreseeable. On the other hand, telling the carrier that it was very important that the shaft be delivered on time would not tell the carrier that the owner would lose money if the shaft was late; there could be other reasons why the owner would need the shaft by a certain time — say, to test out some new machine. I think that the owner would need to say something more in order for the loss to become reasonably foreseeable.

Ashleigh: What if on hearing that promptness was crucial, the carrier raised the price by, say, 30 percent? Does this change anything?

Allie: I think so. That extra 30 percent must have entitled the owner to something. If the carrier charged more when he was told that timeliness was really important, then it seems reasonable to suppose that he was guaranteeing timely delivery and, as part of this guarantee, was assuming the risk of any loss resulting from late delivery.

Andie: I'm not so sure. It's not at all clear that the carrier would be accepting any risk of loss. For all we know, the premium might merely reflect the added costs he would incur in meeting this deadline: perhaps in the overtime he would have to pay. Even if the premium did reflect an assumption of risk, it's unclear precisely what amount of risk the carrier would be accepting—surely he wouldn't be obliged to pay for any and all loss just because he charged extra?

Ashleigh: Yeah, what if it turned out that the owner lost $100 million because this shaft was late—are you saying that the carrier would be liable for this loss simply because he charged an extra 30 percent?

Andie: Hmmm, that does seem odd.

Allie: Maybe you're partially right. The 30 percent probably indicates that there is some transfer of risk here, but I'm not sure how much. It seems difficult to believe that the carrier took on the risk of a $100 million loss.

Andie: So you're suggesting that we have to ask not just whether the *type* of loss was reasonably foreseeable, but whether the *extent* of the loss was reasonably foreseeable? How would that work? Would we apply the *Hadley* v. *Baxendale* test to both questions?

Allie: Sure. We could first ask whether financial loss was reasonably foreseeable, and then ask what amount of loss was reasonably foreseeable. If the owner is going to lose $100 million, then he had better inform the carrier of this. Even if the owner had told the carrier that if the shaft was late his factory would be idle, losing him money, he would have to be explicit about any amount of loss beyond what would ordinarily be expected in these circumstances.

Ashleigh: But aren't these two questions about the type and extent of loss really just two aspects of the same question: What losses were reasonably foreseeable as a consequence of late delivery? In other words, aren't any limits on the extent of loss already implicit in the *Hadley* v. *Baxendale* rule?

Allie: That must be right. Still, asking the two questions separately is helpful in figuring out exactly what losses were reasonably foreseeable.

Andie: A different question just occurred to me. Let's say that the owner specifically told the carrier that he would lose $100,000 if the shaft was delivered late because the factory would be shut down and wouldn't be able to produce certain goods. Now assume that the owner did not actually lose this money because the factory had to be shut down — say, because the order for the goods it was producing was cancelled. But imagine that late delivery caused some other sort of loss — like some government inspector came and since the factory didn't have the shaft the owner was in violation of some regulation and was assessed a $100,000 fine. Should the carrier be liable for $100,000 in that situation?

Ashleigh: Why not? The carrier knew that if he didn't deliver the shaft on time the owner would lose $100,000. That's the type of loss we're dealing with: financial loss. Who cares if that financial loss occurred as a result of the exact concatenation of events contemplated by the parties?

Allie: That seems like kind of a crude way to characterize things to me. The owner chose to be particular about the type of loss that would occur, and he should be held to this. There's not a sufficiently close connection between the owner's loss and the communication between the two parties. At some point, if we choose to characterize things as generally as you suggest, then the only question left will go to the extent of loss.

Andie: I agree. What if the order had not been cancelled and the owner had ended up losing $200,000 — from the factory shutdown *and* the fine. In that case, it seems obvious that the owner would have to eat the fine. Why should the situation be any different just because the order was cancelled?

Ashleigh: Okay, but your argument ignores the fact that the parties agreed to limit recoverable loss to $100,000. Moreover, it begs the question — how do we know that the owner would be eating the fine? Maybe, of the $100,000 he could recover, $50,000 would be for the fine and the other $50,0000 would be for the cancelled order. All we really know is that the amount of loss was limited to $100,000.

Andie: I'm not so sure, Ashleigh — it may seem that way to you, but that's because the way you characterize things ultimately reduces every question to a question about extent of loss.

Ashleigh: Fair enough. But your way of characterizing things seems too limiting: unless the loss exactly matched what the parties specified, it wouldn't be recoverable. If the parties wanted to limit things to a precise concatenation of events, they could have done so. Instead, they left things more general than that.

Allie: But they didn't leave things completely general. What if the owner hadn't said anything to the carrier about the type of loss and had simply stated that if the shaft was late he would lose $100,000. On your theory, the carrier would be liable even in that situation.

Ashleigh: I think so. After all, the carrier knows that a loss of a certain amount will occur. Thus, he should be liable even if the cause of the loss is different from what the owner had expected.

Andie: It seems odd that making a general statement instead of a specific statement allows one a greater scope of recovery.

Ashleigh: Actually, I find that unsurprising. A general statement covers a lot more. If the carrier is worried about loss occurring in any number of different ways, he should charge more to cover off this increased scope of potential loss or else should ask the owner what sort of loss he is worried about to narrow the scope of potential liability.

Andie: Okay guys, let's just move on. In the end, this is just a question of how the phrase "type of loss" should be characterized, and those sorts of question are always difficult to resolve, although the proper characterization probably lies somewhere between these two extremes.

The Benefits of Tiger Spotting

Andie spends a fair amount of time Tiger Spotting in this way because she knows that it yields several benefits. To begin with, it is an especially good way to learn a course because it requires her to actively probe the material. She is not simply treating the facts of cases as so many items in a grocery list, so many bits of meaningless trivia to be memorized, but is carefully sifting through them in an effort to discern their particular significance to the ruling. Because of this she has some sense of how a ruling might change if the facts were slightly altered.

Compare this with Billie's approach. The risk Billie faces is that by simply committing facts to memory he has anchored his understanding of a course in ground that is constantly shifting. When the specific facts change, as they invariably do on an exam, Billie is left adrift in a sea of confusion. The material on which he is being examined appears entirely new and foreign to him. He finds himself looking at a fact pattern that is — by design — surprisingly dissimilar to the cases he thought he had mastered. There is a vague similarity, but the legal facts Billie has stockpiled in his mind are simply not spitting out an answer. The best Billie can do when confronted with such an exam is to write down the legal facts he knows, hoping in this way to impress on the professor that he is a knowledgeable student and, as such, deserves to be rewarded with a good grade.

In contrast, by playing with the facts, Andie has trained her mind to look for the sorts of ambiguity she can expect to find in an exam.

Thus, the exam material is likely to seem less new to her. When the fact pattern on an exam does not quite match those Andie has seen in the cases themselves, she is prepared to discuss alternative characterizations of the new facts before her. Indeed, Andie recognizes that part of what is involved in writing a successful exam is that she point out the ways in which the given facts are ambiguous: that is, similar in some ways, but dissimilar in others, to the facts that drive the rulings. Based on how she characterizes ambiguous facts, or how much emphasis she places on these respective similarities or dissimilarities, Andie is able to develop creative arguments for how the fact pattern should be resolved. Even when an argument is ultimately misguided, Andie knows that it is sometimes worth making (and refuting) on an exam, if for no other reason than to indicate to the professor that she understands the nature of the "game" that is being played.

"You cover hundreds of cases in first year Contracts — you have to know them like the back of your hand!"

In this respect, Andie once again differentiates herself from Billie. For Billie, thinking that the object of the law exam game is to display brute knowledge, does not center his exam answer on creative arguments based on subtle characterizations of the facts, but on categorical rules he can apply to any set of facts (or so he thinks). Andie knows that it is dangerous to see cases as laying down categorical rules, or absolute principles, when the rulings in those cases are being driven by a particular set of facts. She is therefore constantly on the lookout for arguments based on factual characterizations that bring into question the application of rules set down in the case law.

This is not to say that Andie is indiscriminate in the kinds of arguments she will run on an exam. She will not, of course, make just any old argument based on an outrageous characterization of some relatively unimportant fact. The trick is to know whether there's actually a bit of room to make the argument or whether making the argument will instead only serve to show she doesn't properly understand the course material. Picking and prodding at

86

the facts in the cases — Tiger Spotting — has helped prepare Andie to discriminate in this way. By asking how the outcome of a given case might change if certain facts were different Andie has determined which facts are most crucial to the ruling and, thus, determined the (often narrow) principle that is at the heart of the ruling.

There are, moreover, other ancillary benefits that Andie gets from Tiger Spotting. For one, by playing around with the facts of cases, Andie is sometimes able to anticipate one or more of the twists that the professor will throw into his own exam fact pattern. This is the most direct and obvious way in which Tiger Spotting ensures that the exam appears less "new" to Andie. When she sees a variation on the facts of a case that she and her friends already anticipated and discussed as a group, she is well placed to deal with it.

More commonly, however, Tiger Spotting assists Andie in making her High Level Summary, because it ensures that she has already spent time considering what is most important about any given case. We will discuss the High Level Summary in more detail shortly. For now, it suffices to point out that making a High Level Summary requires that Andie boil a case down to its essential "bottom line", and that Tiger Spotting is of tremendous help in this regard.

Story Telling

Tiger Spotting is all about being alive to difference, or being able to identify when slight changes or alterations in a set of facts may limit the application of a legal rule. This is an important exam-writing skill. However, it is not enough, by itself, to ensure that Andie will get an A on her exam. Consider our basketball analogy once again. There is more to "reading the play" in basketball than merely being able to tell the difference between a pick and roll and a back-door play. One also needs to know how each of these plays fits into the coach's overall offensive scheme. When is it appropriate to run one of these plays as opposed to the other? Can they be run together, as part of a complex half-court attack? In short, how do these plays *relate* to one another as well as to the overall system? Similar considerations go into reading the play in a law exam.

To ask such questions is, after all, to ask questions about how details should be synthesized, or systematized. Whether one is talking about plays in an offensive scheme, or cases in a field of law, Andie pays special attention to such questions. Indeed, we have, throughout the preceding, emphasized the importance of synthesis to Andie's overall approach to law school. Story Telling is a study technique that Andie employs to hone the important skill of synthesizing individual cases — learning to understand them under unifying concepts — in preparation for the exam.

To begin to see how Story Telling works, think back to one of our earlier recurring examples: our grocery list example from chapter 1. There we suggested that by using a unifying concept like "cake" to sort the detailed items on a grocery list one could get a sense of both: (1) which items on the list were most important; and (2) what the functions of all the various items were. This meant that one could quite reasonably forego a mental checklist altogether, simply by knowing that one needed certain items to form the cake's batter, certain items to give it flavour, and so forth.

Now consider the syllabus of a typical law school course. The course will be divided up under a number of different headings that describe general topics or subtopics. Under each heading there will be a sequence of cases, one of which is likely to be the "leading case." The goal of Story Telling is to sort the cases under these various headings — "Consequential Loss," for example — in much the same way as one might sort the items on a grocery list under the concept "cake." Just as each item on the grocery list could be seen to be performing a special function once that list was understood under the concept "cake," Andie knows that her professor has a special reason for including each case that appears under the heading "Consequential Loss". Moreover, he often has a special reason for including them in the exact order that he does. Determining what these special reasons are through Story Telling will give Andie a sense of the specific function of each case in the law of consequential loss.

In practice, Story Telling works in the following manner. Andie and her friends take turns trying to spin a yarn that ties together the cases under a given heading. Each person must, without much reference to the particular facts of the case (which would muddle the basic story they are trying to tell with unnecessary details), provide a narrative for the group of cases. This involves attempting to discuss the cases in order, focusing on how they relate to one another.

Typically, the cases will build on and refine one another. Andie and her friends ask how each case in the sequence adds to the ones that came before it. Does the case give a new rationale for an existing rule? Does it address an ambiguity that was previously latent in the case law? Does it reinterpret the cases that came before it? Explicitly asking these questions helps Andie and her friends to piece together how the legal equivalents of "cakes" are constructed.

And this, in turn, helps to develop their theoretical understanding of law — their ability to see the big picture, to grasp law as a coherent whole that is tied together under unifying categories and concepts. Of course, not every yarn they spin will be as helpful as every other in this regard. Sometimes it may even seem that a story that was supposed to be about "cake" is more suited to describing "lasagna," as it were. But that's no cause for concern. Andie and her friends know that sometimes their theoretical understanding of the law is developed as much by these failed efforts (and the exercise of determining why they failed) as by more successful attempts at Story Telling.

Of particular importance to the Story Telling exercise, not surprisingly, is the preferred theoretical approach to law of Andie's professor. As we explained in chapter 1, since it is he who will ultimately grade the exam, Andie knows she must go out of her way to understand the cases — and, more specifically, how they fit together or relate to one another — as he does. Wherever possible, Andie therefore spins her yarns in the light of his theory. Of course, if her professor does not have such a theory — if, in other words, he is Doctor Doctrine — or if he has a theory that does a poor job of explaining the cases, Andie can always fall back on using her own preferred theoretical framework in Story Telling. Even if this theoretical framework cannot be used on an exam, it will provide her with many of the independent benefits of synthetic understanding.

To remind ourselves, those benefits are both mnemonic (since, by understanding the cases in relation to one another, it is far less likely that Andie will fail to recall any single case on an exam) and organizational. Because of her synthetic understanding, Andie is able to process and sort "new" details with great facility. Thus, when Andie is confronted with a factual twist on a legal issue — the legal equivalent of a substitution of mayonnaise for vegetable oil in her recipe for cake — she is able to easily determine how, if at all, that twist alters her basic story about the relevant area of the law. Like Andie's other strategies, Story Telling thus helps to ensure that nothing on an exam is ever *really* all that "new" to her.

The alternative to reaping these kinds of benefits from Story Telling is to simply memorize a hodgepodge of seemingly random and disconnected points from various cases. This, as we know, is essentially Billie's approach to the studying. Unfortunately for Billie, he is so concerned with memorizing facts and other such details that he misses the bigger picture almost entirely. In contrast, Andie knows that details are only useful insofar as they help fill in this bigger picture. On their own, they simply take up valuable space in her head that is better allocated to remembering the lyrics to her favourite songs.

The Association Game

Ideally, Andie and her friends could tell stories that would synthesize, not only the cases under a discrete heading or subheading of the course, but all the cases comprising the course as a whole. Even assuming that their level of synthetic understanding were so complete (which is what they always aspire to, if not what they always attain) there would be practical difficulties standing in the way of this. Such a story would be more akin to an epic — an extended treatise, really — than to the kind of campfire tales Story Telling is intended to elicit. This would not only interfere with the enjoyment of the group's exam preparation experience; it would also tax its valuable time excessively. In view of this, Andie and her friends turn to another studying technique in order to acquire practice synthesizing across headings or topics covered in the course: the Association Game.

We can best introduce this game by comparing it to a popular children's game that involves drawing connections between the names of U.S. states on the basis of the letters that form their names. The idea is to use the *last* letter in the name of one state to think of another state whose name *begins* with that letter. If one child names "Washington," for example, the next child might name "Nebraska," followed by another child naming "Arkansas," and so forth. The game ends when one of the children cannot think of a state name beginning with the appropriate letter.

The Association Game is quite similar to this, with the exception that its object is to associate something less banal than letters of the alphabet: principles and arguments. Andie's game works by having one member of the group pick a case and draw some connection between it and a case from another section of the course. That connection can consist of anything from a theoretical idea that is expressed in both cases, to a common judicial mindset, to a similarity of doctrinal significance. Once one member of the group has taken a stab at doing this, another member of the group picks up where she left off: comparing or contrasting the second case with a case from still another section. In between each person's turn, the group will usually have a brief discussion about the connection drawn, critically assessing whether it is an important one, and suggesting other connections that might have been drawn. Where the connection is either too tenuous or obvious (and a certain degree of latitude is usually appropriate here), Andie and her friends will not hesitate to mock one another. After all, nothing negatively reinforces a bad argument quite as effectively as laughing and pointing.

As this last comment suggests, The Association Game (like Story Telling) is not only intended to be an effective technique for synthesizing material: it is also meant to be amusing. Making a game out of studying and going back and forth with friends is immeasurably more enjoyable than sitting by oneself in some dingy corner of the library, struggling through anxiety and lapses in concentration. It is therefore relatively easy for Andie to spend hours at a time studying in this manner.

The High Level Summary

Walk into any exam room and look at what people have on their desks. A great number of them will undoubtedly have tabbed up textbooks and eighty-page summaries in front of them, all of which have been highlighted with coloured markers so that the material resembles a psychedelic portrait better suited to a fifteen-year-old's room than a law school exam. These people are Billies. It is unsurprising that Billie has reams of paper in front of him—after all, people bring into the exam what they think they need. Since Billie thinks that he needs to know a vast array of facts, he brings a vast array of factual information.

Andie, on the other hand, knows that she needs a high-level understanding of the course, and so she brings a High Level Summary into the exam. A High Level Summary is a summary of the course which consists of one succinct comment on each case. Because of its succinctness, Andie is able to see, at a glance, what the course is all about without getting lost in the details. This is the equivalent of having an aerial view of the forest. The idea is to have the name and the description of each case take up no more than one or two lines. In the end, Andie's High Level is typically no more than half a dozen pages in length.

"My summary for Contracts was 135 pages—it had everything in it!"

Billie would feel naked walking into an exam with such a short summary. But Andie is confident, for she knows that the exam will not require her to know many details and, in any case, there is not enough time in an exam to flip through an eighty-page summary looking for some case she vaguely recalls is somewhere in it. Because of its length, the High Level Summary is very easy to navigate and Andie is very familiar with it. Andie may bring additional material to the exam, if for no other reason than for the sake of having a security blanket, but the occasions on which she will have to refer to this material will be few and far between.

As important as it is to have a good High Level Summary in an exam, an even greater benefit lies in the process of making such a summary. The thought process involved in distilling a case to its essential elements is invaluable. At the most basic level, this has the effect of engaging Andie's mind so that she is not passively skimming through her material. More importantly, asking what is truly essential about a case cannot help but advance one's understanding of it. Making a High Level Summary forces Andie to question which facts and arguments are central to the case and which are of secondary importance.

In preparing her High Level Summary Andie starts with the more extensive summary she has been using all semester. She thinks back to the discussions she had with her group about each case. Given that she can write only a line (or perhaps two) about each case, what should it be? She thinks about what information she would need to remind herself of if she drew a blank during the exam. She settles on what she thinks is essential and writes it down. She might also put some keywords in her summary to trigger her memory about the facts or an especially significant argument that she and her friends came up with when discussing the case. If, for example, she was summarizing *Hadley* v. *Baxendale* she might write:

> *Hadley* v. *Baxendale*: shaft late; 2 prt test — ordinary or special loss; consider type *and* extent of loss

Notice that most of the points that came up when Andie and her friends were playing with facts did not make it into the High Level Summary. Those points are useful and will stick in her head, but they are not essential.

Asking what is most significant about each case is particularly important in the days immediately preceding the exam. Andie's task at this time is to bring her understanding of the course into focus. Accordingly, she is less concerned with the sort of free-ranging discussion that characterized much of her studying to this point and is more concerned with deciding which of the insights gleaned from these discussions are the most important for exam purposes. This is not to suggest that the process of making a High Level Summary is somehow disconnected from Andie's previous study techniques. As discussed, techniques such as the Page Flip, Tiger Spotting, Story Telling, and The Association Game all helped Andie arrive at the understanding she is now trying to summarize. In other words, these techniques helped Andie get to the stage where she is able to generate a good High Level Summary.

Once Andie has made her High Level Summary she works with it, editing it and learning to navigate her way through it. Doing this makes it much easier for her to find what she is looking for in her summary during the exam. Working with her High Level Summary also affords Andie another opportunity to synthesize information. Because she can see an entire section of the course summarized on less than a single page, and take it all in at a glance, Andie is presented with a golden opportunity to make connections between the cases that she might have otherwise missed.

Practice Exams

Taking practice exams is a widely used study technique. Indeed, Billie will undoubtedly schedule four or five practice exams into his study routine. Unfortunately, Billie uses practice exams in the wrong way. He views them as trial runs, not as an opportunity to develop his understanding of the course in the context of a new set of facts. He may even go so far as to lock himself in his room and write numerous practice exams under timed conditions.

What, one might wonder, is Billie getting out of this experience? Aside from an ulcer and prematurely grey hair, the only thing Billie acquires by taking practice exams in this manner is some experience taking exams under simulated conditions. This may be of some benefit to do once in one's law school career, if only to accustom oneself to the experience. However, it is difficult to see how doing this repeatedly is of any value; it is easy to see how doing this repeatedly is remarkably painful.

Recognizing this, Andie approaches practice exams differently. She knows that the point of the exercise is not to practise writing for three hours, but to get a better sense of what sort of issues are likely to arise on the exam and how best to handle them. In other words, Andie uses practice exams as another vehicle to develop her Tiger Spotting skills and to practise applying her professor's preferred theory to a particular set of facts. Accordingly, whenever possible, Andie ensures that she uses a practice exam written by her professor. A practice exam written by another professor, while still useful, will be of lesser benefit since it is likely designed to elicit ideas that are relevant to that other professor's preferred theory.

As always, Andie does not engage in this study technique in isolation: she collaborates with her friends. Moreover, she and her friends approach practice exams in a way that makes full use of the benefits of collaboration. This involves taking a bit of time to individually read the fact pattern and jot down some initial thoughts. Each of them takes a first stab at spotting the issues and considering how particular facts may be used to argue in favour of one resolution or another. All this should take no more than ten minutes. Following this, Andie and her friends open the floor for discussion. This is where they start to pick up Big Bills. They share their respective insights, critically evaluating each. They attempt to draw connections between and build on these various insights. As a group, they comb over the fact pattern again to see if they have missed anything. The

Take It to the BANK: Big Bills for STUDYING

$ Collaborate—as always, do most of your work with your friends.

$ Learn the nuts and bolts of the course by doing a Page Flip.

$ Tiger Spot—play with the facts of cases.

$ Train yourself to be attuned to ambiguity.

$ Seek synthesis within particular sections of the course by Story Telling.

$ Seek synthesis among different sections of the course by playing The Association Game.

$ Make a High Level Summary and refine it.

$ Discuss practice exams with your group to hone specific skills.

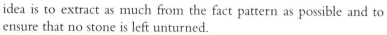

idea is to extract as much from the fact pattern as possible and to ensure that no stone is left unturned.

Among the benefits of this exercise is that it affords Andie a critical sounding board for her own response to the exam. This ensures that Andie does not make heavy weather of relatively insignificant facts or pursue red herrings. As well, she gets an opportunity to see how others would handle the same set of facts. If one of her friends sees a subtle issue or uses a fact in a way that Andie would not have considered, Andie will be more attuned to this sort of thing when writing the real exam. In connection with this last point, doing practice exams with a group ensures that there are no significant holes in Andie's doctrinal knowledge or understanding of the course. Alarm bells will go off if Andie misses an issue that all her friends saw or fails to recognize an opportunity that others seize to wax theoretical for her professor.

More mundanely, Andie gains insight into what sort of exam her professor tends to write. Like the rest of us, professors are creatures of habit, and if Andie's professor found an issue worth examining in past years there is a good chance he will find it worth examining this year. This is especially true in relation to theoretical issues. Professors invariably set exams that bring out the essential elements of their theory. In an exam set by The Politician, for example, Andie can be sure that questions involving competing social values will arise. Similarly, Andie knows that issues of efficiency will be lurking behind any exam set by The Economist. To prepare to address these more theoretical aspects of the exam, Andie and her group use the practice exam to gain experience applying their professor's theory to a given set of facts. This is similar to what they were doing when they were trying to explain cases in light of their professor's theory in the course of doing the Page Flip. The difference is that now they are applying this theory to a hypothetical situation designed by their professor. Since he designed it, Andie knows with certainty that his pet issues will find their way into it.

A POSTSCRIPT:
What SHOULD I Do If I Start Studying LATE?

At some point in one's law school career one may find oneself woefully underprepared and with just a few days to learn the material before the exam. Many students who find themselves with such a limited amount of time to learn what appears to be a mountain of information are overcome with anxiety and try to mimic what they see Billie doing. Charlie often makes this mistake. For two days, or however long Charlie has, he will bury himself in his books and try to finagle an invite to Billie's study group. He will drink countless cups of coffee trying to stave off sleep, hoping that he will somehow stumble onto some shortcut to becoming Billie. Unfortunately, as we have seen, there are no shortcuts to becoming Billie. Indeed, part of what it is to be Billie is to deny the possibility of shortcuts. Consequently, this sort of short-term Billieness is likely to give Charlie detailed knowledge of some parts of the course, with no idea of what is going on in other parts. In the end, this will leave Charlie nothing more than a poor-man's Billie. How can one do better?

While doing nothing until a few days before the exam is obviously not an Andie strategy, it is still possible to implement an Andie strategy if one finds oneself in this unfortunate situation. To understand how and why this is so, two facts must be recognized. First, one is not going to learn everything. It is simply too late for that. Second, one can take solace in the fact that the concept of diminishing marginal returns applies to studying. When studying, one's largest gains are made during the first several hours. As time goes on and one's studying becomes increasingly detail oriented, one makes smaller gains per hour. To be sure, these smaller gains are useful and possibly even necessary to get an A. Still, if one has only a couple of days to learn the whole course, one can put oneself in a good position to salvage a decent grade assuming one focuses on the right material. The question then, is what to focus on?

To begin with, one must recognize that there will not be time to implement all the techniques that we have outlined in this chapter. Consequently, one should focus on the techniques that can be used to develop a basic understanding of the course. Story Telling and The Association Game are all about developing a sophisticated understanding of the course. When all one has time for is obtaining a working knowledge of the basic elements of the course, these techniques should be put aside. The techniques that should still be utilized are a modified version of The Page Flip, Tiger Spotting, and the High Level Summary.

The Page Flip should be used to gain a working knowledge of the core concepts and cases. However, where one is under greater time constraints, one should forego examining every case and concentrate on the more important or "leading" cases. Cases that are included for context or to show the development of a principle that is articulated in a leading case should be ignored in order to free up time to think about the leading cases. One can still do some Tiger Spotting with respect to these cases, but again this must necessarily be truncated. Instead of the free-ranging Tiger Spotting one would normally engage in, one should ask how the outcome might have been different if one or two facts were different. Because one faces diminishing marginal returns, one is better off asking only a few of these sorts of questions about any given case before moving on to do the same with the next case. As well, there will likely only be time for one Page Flip. We recommend doing one relatively thorough Page Flip, focusing on the more important cases, rather than attempting to cram in two rushed Page Flips.

Another technique that remains essential (and arguably becomes even more important) when one has only a short period within which to learn the course is to prepare a High Level Summary. Where one has only a few days to learn the course, it is crucial to have a summary that can be easily navigated during the exam. Similarly, the benefits of preparing a High Level Summary are more pronounced when one is forced to "cram" for an exam. Since one of the challenges in learning a course in a short period of time is becoming familiar with a great deal of information, an exercise that forces one to focus on what is most essential about this information is extremely helpful.

Of course, making a High Level Summary will be more difficult where one has not had the benefit of in-depth discussions of the cases and exercises such as Story Telling and the Association Game. Instead of selecting the most significant insights from one's previous studying, one will have to decide what is essential about a case from a less informed perspective. However, one may take comfort in the fact that diminishing marginal returns are operative here too: the process of making a High Level Summary is of even greater benefit to one who is cramming than it is to one who has already developed a solid understanding of the course. In part, this is due to the fact that preparing and studying from a High Level Summary allows one to synthesize, or make connections between the cases, without doing so at the expense of learning the nuts and bolts of the course. This is particularly important for the crammer, who does not have time to do both using separate exercises.

four

The Exam

AFTER months of practice, the big day finally arrives. The morning of the exam finds our three protagonists in different moods. Charlie wakes up feeling tired. He had a restless night, tossing and turning and asking why he ever turned his back on Billieness. He wanders into his living room and stares regretfully at the empty pizza box and cans of beer adorning his coffee table. He sees his panicky and guilty eyes in the mirror and worries that today he shall meet his comeuppance.

Billie, for his part, had a restful sleep. He wakes up at the scheduled time and eats his usual meal of cereal, juice, half a banana, and a single soft-boiled egg. He admiringly studies his half-bearded visage in the mirror. He flexes his writing hand and tells himself he's got nothing to worry about. "After all," he says to himself, "with all the blood I've spilt, how can I lose?"

Like Billie, Andie wakes up feeling good about what she has done up to this point. Like Charlie, she is not convinced that this will be enough to guarantee her a good grade. Unlike either of her less evolved counterparts, Andie realizes that the exam involves more than simply playing out the events that have already been set in motion to their natural conclusion. Andie knows that for the coming three hours she must continue to do what she has done all term: implement the proper system. This is the primary difference between Andie and the other characters on exam day: Andie is the only one who believes that strategy and decision-making still matter.

The mistake Billie and Charlie make is the one they have been making all semester long—they do not think strategically. They accept the conventional wisdom that exam success is strictly a product of intelligence and hard work, and they put their faith (or despair in Charlie's case) in this fact.

The basis for this misunderstanding lies in their view of what a law school exam is really about. For Billie, an exam is a "test," in the general sense. It is a challenge to his self-worth, a death struggle in which his detailed knowledge of the course material is pitted against a fact pattern.

"When you walk into the exam room, *alea jacta est*, my friend — the die is cast! Your grade is now in the hands of fate."

Taking Law School EXAMS

For Charlie, a law school exam is a "test" in the pejorative sense — the way it is a test when his girlfriend asks him to forego a night on the couch watching the *Star Wars* tetralogy for the umpteenth time to attend a dinner party with her friends. Charlie mistakenly views both this request and the exam as cruel and arbitrary impositions that seek to destroy his happiness to prove some meaningless point.

Andie differs from the other two characters in that she does not see the ultimate goal of law school exams in terms of proving a point. Exams do not test intelligence. Nor do they test one's work ethic. They simply test how well one handles the course material from within the perspective of the professor's preferred theory. Accordingly, for Andie, a law school exam is a vehicle through which to communicate to her professor that she understands his view of the course.

Unsurprisingly, the way each character understands exams influences how each writes exams. Charlie's belief that he needs to defeat the exam by the application of knowledge causes him to take a fatalistic approach. He is resigned to a bad grade, as he believes it is too late to do anything about it (and in a sense it is, though there are certainly things he can still do to help himself). When he gets into the exam room he will do his best to sound knowledgeable and intelligent, but without substantive knowledge or any framework with which to generate insights his answer is likely doomed to be scattered, unreflective, and vague.

Billie understands exams in much the same way as Charlie and reacts in a similar, though more successful, fashion. Because Billie has mastered the details of the course, he is able to use the exam as a launching pad to show his superior knowledge. If a fact pattern raises a particular issue, Billie will seize this opportunity to drop all that he knows about this area of the law in order to signal to his professor "look—I *know* this."

In contrast, Andie knows that her professor will not be impressed by trivia masquerading as insight. Instead, she realizes that he wants to see a higher-level grasp of the material demonstrated. Accordingly, Andie looks for ways to show that she understands the connections between various elements of the course. There are several ways in which this can be accomplished. For one, where Billie drops knowledge Andie drops understanding. This is relatively easy for Andie given that when she and her friends were studying for the exam, they developed brief, high level explanations of each subsection of the course. These explanations were developed through techniques such as Story Telling. On the exam, Andie searches for opportunities to drop these pithy one-liners to signal to her professor "look—I *understand* this."

Another way in which Andie communicates to her professor that she understands the material is by pointing out connections between various cases and sections of the course. Andie does not have to discover these connections on the spot—she and her friends spent time searching for them when they were playing The Association Game.

Finally, Andie is able to communicate to her professor that she understands the course because she is not confused by the "newness" of the exam. Some professors are notorious for devising strange and intricate fact patterns that diverge from the facts of the cases that have been studied. Billie's difficulty is that because his knowledge of the course is anchored in its details, when these details inevitably change, his knowledge fails him. He suddenly finds that while he knows a great deal about the cases he read, he knows very little about the fact pattern confronting him. Andie, because she understands the course at a higher level of abstraction, does not face this problem to the same degree. For Andie, the course was never really about its minutia, so when the facts change she does not have the proverbial rug pulled out from under her the way Billie does.

The preceding discussion is directed at considerations specifically relevant to the law school exam. Andie appreciates that the law school exam is a unique creature, but she also realizes that the same rules that apply to any exam also apply to a law school exam. Accordingly, Andie ensures that she has an organized answer that is fully responsive to the question asked. If Billie and Charlie are smart, even they will have latched on to these insights.

Still, they may not have latched on to precisely what this requires in the context of law exams. Even though Andie knows that a law exam tests one's understanding of the professor's theory, she also knows that this understanding has to be played out in the context of the fact pattern. Thus, she will refrain from going off on theoretical tangents and will stay close to the facts as much as possible. Andie realizes that in a law exam the facts are the question, or, more accurately, the question is implicit in the facts. This means one must be careful to understand exactly which problems are posed by the facts. Too often, students jump into an answer without first identifying and fully articulating the appropriate question. Andie has two main ways of ensuring that this does not happen: she reads the fact pattern twice and she makes an outline.

Reading the Fact Pattern Twice

Andie derives three primary benefits from reading fact patterns twice. First, it provides her with time to consider the fact pattern and allow her thoughts to percolate before writing her answer. Many students dive into their answers headfirst in response to the time constraints imposed on them. The danger here is that if one does not take adequate time to formulate a plan of attack, one's answer is likely to be disorganized and incomplete.

A second benefit of reading fact patterns twice is that it ensures Andie does not miss "the forest for the trees." It is sometimes difficult to fully appreciate the significance of any given fact without knowing where the story is going. Having read the fact pattern once,

Andie has a sense of the overall picture when she reads it again. One of the ways Andie distinguishes herself is by using information from one part of the fact pattern in her discussion of an issue arising in another part. It is much easier for Andie to make these sorts of connections on a second read, as she has all the issues contained in the fact pattern in mind.

A third benefit is that reading the fact pattern twice allows Andie to "catch more". If Andie does not want to lose the forest for the trees, she is equally concerned to ensure that she does not fail to take note of each individual tree. The first time Andie reads the fact pattern she tries to spot the main issues, jotting down her initial thoughts but not worrying too much if she does not recognize every issue. The second time Andie reads the fact pattern she makes a conscious effort to go over it with a fine-toothed comb, asking why each piece of information contained in the fact pattern is there. Explicitly asking this question is helpful, as many an A has been lost by overlooking an important issue.

Making an Outline

A second tactic Andie employs to ensure that she properly identifies and articulates the appropriate question is to make an outline. As with reading the fact pattern twice, this affords her more time to develop her thoughts. More important, using an outline helps her structure her answer in an organized manner. An organized answer makes it easier for Andie's professor to follow her reasoning and it goes a long way to creating the impression that she is a systematic thinker. For these reasons, an answer that goes through each issue methodically is superior to one that jumps back and forth between issues. Sometimes when one is writing an answer, a thought that properly belongs with an issue that arose previously does not come to mind until after one has finished discussing that issue. Other times, the thought will have occurred to one at the outset, but it will not be until one starts putting one's thoughts down on paper that one appreciates which part of the answer in which it belongs. While it is impossible to eliminate these problems, making an outline can help minimize them. Doing so forces one to think about how each argument and fact relates to the overall structure of one's answer.

To prepare an outline Andie makes rough notes of the issues that she spots as she reads the fact pattern for the first time. She makes further notes the second time that she reads the fact pattern. At this point, she organizes her notes into subheadings addressing the main issues. She now has a structure within which to construct her answer that helps her deal with each issue in a discrete and organized manner. This structure also makes it easier for her to comment on the overlap between different issues so that she can demonstrate to her professor that she understands not only each issue unto itself but also the connections between various issues.

While making her outline, Andie jots down the names of any cases she wants to discuss so that she does not forget to raise them. If she does not recall the name of a case or wants to check to make sure that she has not overlooked anything important, Andie refers to her High Level Summary. People are often concerned about relying on their summaries too much in an exam. Although flipping through a summary can eat precious minutes, this problem is alleviated by Andie's approach. Because she uses a High Level Summary, she can quickly look something up, both because there are so few pages to flip through and because the summary is so brief that she has intimate knowledge of its contents.

Further, Andie is not overly concerned about spending a bit of time looking things up, just as she is not worried about the time it takes her to read the fact pattern twice and make an outline. Losing time is something that Billie and Charlie are more concerned with because they think they need as much time as they can get to fill the exam booklet with evidence of their knowledge. Andie recognizes that it is more important for an exam to be thoughtful than comprehensive and so is willing to spend a bit more time getting ready to write.

The Content of the Exam: Using IDAR

Of course, to know how to plan an exam answer is not yet to know how to begin filling in the *content* of that answer. But here too Andie has a systematic approach to law exams that is of great assistance to her. Just as Andie reads the fact pattern twice and makes an outline in order to ensure that she properly identifies and articulates the question being asked, so she uses another heuristic—IDAR—in order to ensure that she adequately addresses that question, that her answer to it has the proper content.

By itself, this does nothing to distinguish Andie from her less developed counterparts. Indeed, IDAR is widely recognized as setting out a useful methodology for filling out the content of one's exam answers. Even Charlie has heard this acronym, and knows what it stands for: Issue, Doctrine, Ambiguity, and Resolution. But how is this acronym to be properly applied in practice? "Well," Billie might explain, "when you're writing an exam, you have to spot the *issues*, connect them to the *doctrine*, show how the facts highlight *ambiguities* in the doctrine, and arrive at some *resolution*." Billie's mechanical recitation of the literal meaning of the acronym may be correct, but it misses out on what is most essential about IDAR.

Implicit in Billie's approach to IDAR is the assumption that all four elements that make up the acronym deserve equal attention on an exam. In fact, this is not the case. It is certainly true that a law school exam requires one to spot issues and connect them to doctrine. But one could only arrive at the conclusion that these elements of the acronym get at the essence of what law school exams test by adopting Billie's assumption that the best way to succeed in law school is through brute memorization and regurgitation.

Of course, Andie rejects that assumption. Her own view, as we have seen, is that law school success is largely premised on one's ability to understand, and make arguments from, the preferred perspective or approach to law of her various professors. This has immediate implications for her understanding of IDAR. For one thing, it implies that Andie's strategy in using IDAR should be continuously adapted to reflect these approaches. For another, it implies that in Andie's view the most important element of IDAR is the one that calls not for a display of mere knowledge and ability to regurgitate, but for an appropriate display of understanding and argumentation.

As it turns out, that element is *ambiguity*. In fact, no matter which type of professor she is writing for, a significant portion of Andie's exam answer—often the lion's share—is devoted to dealing with factual ambiguity, the sort of ambiguity that gets raised when "new" facts in the exam fact pattern differ slightly from the facts that drive the rulings themselves. However much her professors might differ in other respects, they are quite similar with respect to their tendency to pack their exams with such factual ambiguity. Andie takes this to be *ipso facto* evidence that they all consider it to be of great importance. And because Andie's exercises in Tiger Spotting were designed to help her identify and deal with these sorts of ambiguities, she is amply prepared to accord this element of IDAR the level of importance it deserves in her exam answer. Relying on her Tiger Spotting experience, Andie structures her exam answer around creative arguments based on subtle characterizations of ambiguous facts.

This is not to say that her treatment of ambiguity does not differ from professor to professor. For Andie knows that one man's ambiguity is another man's red herring. Thus, what may constitute an ambiguity for The Politician, with his focus on context and social policy, will often be nothing of the sort for The Philosopher, with his focus on universal principle and his rejection of instrumentalism. Andie remains constantly alive to these differences in her respective professors even as she recognizes the importance of ambiguity to all of them in general.

Differences in her professors' approaches to law also cause Andie to make adjustments in terms of how she handles other elements of IDAR. For example, because Doctor Doctrine focuses on the importance of doctrine, Andie is likely to spend more time covering as many issues and as much doctrine as possible when writing an exam for him. Meanwhile, The Politician's instrumentalism entails that, for him, the element of resolution is more important than it is for others. In one sense, the appropriate resolution — the desired social goal or policy — must drive Andie's legal analysis of issues from the outset if she is to provide The Politician with an ideal exam answer. Knowing this, Andie spends more time thinking and writing about the correct resolution to an issue in any exam written for him.

Sample Exam

To demonstrate Andie's approach to writing exams, let's go through, step by step, how she might deal with a sample fact pattern. Our sample fact pattern deals only with the *Hadley* v. *Baxendale* doctrine of consequential loss. Admittedly, this is somewhat artificial because exams require one to disentangle and deal with a number of issues involving different (albeit sometimes related) doctrines. However, the exercise of writing a real exam will be substantially similar, if somewhat more complex.

Included in what follows is Andie's marked-up copy of the fact pattern as it would appear after she has read it twice, as well as her outline. The sample answer is written for The Philosopher. Following Andie's answer we provide a "Post-Game Analysis" in which we break down her answer paragraph by paragraph and discuss which "plays" worked and why. Each paragraph of Andie's answer has been numbered for ease of reference in the post-game analysis.

As part of this post-game analysis, we also provide alternative analyses of selected issues for other types of professors. These alternative analyses are not meant to supplant the answer Andie has provided for The Philosopher. There would be considerable overlap between the two, given that we have assumed the same facts and that legal doctrine remains constant regardless of the person for whom one is writing. Nevertheless, there are significant differences in the kind of exam Andie would write for The Economist, say, as opposed to The Philosopher, and the point of these alternative analyses is to indicate what some of these differences might be. Note that the fact that this exam only addresses one case and doctrine limits our ability to provide guidance on the sort of answer Andie would write for Doctor Doctrine. For, as we have seen, Doctor Doctrine is especially eager to see connections drawn between the fact pattern and as many different cases and doctrines as possible.

Sample Fact Pattern

In 1998 the Hugs Foundation hired Corbin Contracting to build a "Millennium Castle," which Hugs intended to use to host a New Year's Eve fundraising event for indigent Law Professors. Hugs told Corbin the name of the proposed castle and what it was to be used for before entering into the contract.

Beginning in 1999, Hugs sold tickets to the event for $10,000 each. The 500 tickets available sold out within three days. On the tickets Hugs included a promise to refund the ticket price if, for whatever reason, the event was cancelled. Hugs proceeded to inform

Corbin of the price of the tickets and the number sold. Hugs also stated that if the castle was not completed on time it would be necessary to pay out "millions" in refunds.

The blueprints clearly indicated that the highlight of the castle was to be two large turrets. To build the turrets, Corbin hired Chitty Contracting Inc., a much smaller company specializing in medieval architecture and construction. Prior to entering into the contract Corbin said to Chitty, "It's absolutely crucial that these turrets be completed by December 20th as they are needed for a New Year's Eve party. How much is this going to cost me?" Chitty replied, "This job would usually cost $2,000. Given your time constraints, I have to charge a premium of, let's say, 20 percent. So the total cost will be $2,400." Corbin agreed to these terms.

The turrets were not completed in time because Chitty dedicated its resources toward a more profitable project, from which it earned an extra $10,000.

Because the castle was not completed on time, Hugs had to refund all the tickets it had sold. As a result, Hugs ceased operations and is no longer carrying on charitable activities. Hugs is suing Corbin for its consequential loss of $5 million. Corbin in turn is suing Chitty.

Analyze the likely outcome of each lawsuit.

Andie's Marked Up Fact Pattern

[handwritten: once in a lifetime]

In 1998 the Hugs Foundation hired Corbin Contracting to build a "Millennium Castle," *[handwritten: charity - tickets likely expensive]* which Hugs intended to use to host a New Year's Eve fundraising event for indigent Law Professors. Hugs told Corbin the name of the proposed castle and what it was to be used for before entering into the contract. *[handwritten: what can be inferred from this?]*

Beginning in 1999, Hugs sold tickets to the event for $10,000 each. The 500 tickets available sold out within three days. On the tickets Hugs included a promise to refund *[handwritten: did Corbin know]* the ticket price if, for whatever reason, the event was cancelled. Hugs proceeded to inform Corbin of the price of the tickets and the number sold. Hugs also stated that if the *[handwritten: communicated after formation]* castle was not completed on time it would be necessary to pay out "millions" in refunds.

[handwritten: All parties presumably knew this]

The blueprints clearly indicated that the highlight of the castle was to be two large turrets. To build the turrets, Corbin hired Chitty Contracting Inc., a much smaller company specializing in medieval architecture and construction. Prior to entering into the contract Corbin said to Chitty, "It's absolutely crucial that these turrets be completed by *[handwritten: what did this tell Chitty?]* December 20th as they are needed for a New Year's Eve party. How much is this going to cost me?" Chitty replied, "This job would usually cost $2,000. Given your time constraints, I have to charge a premium of, let's say, 20 percent. So the total cost will be *[handwritten: Chitty informed of importance of timeliness]* $2,400." Corbin agreed to these terms. *[handwritten: was this an assumption of risk?]*

The turrets were not completed in time because Chitty dedicated its resources toward a more profitable project, from which it earned an extra $10,000. *[handwritten: does this matter?]*

Because the castle was not completed on time, Hugs had to refund all the tickets it had *[handwritten: was this loss reasonably foreseeable - Hadley v. Baxendal]* sold. As a result, Hugs ceased operations and is no longer carrying on charitable activities. Hugs is suing Corbin for its consequential loss of $5 million. Corbin in turn is suing Chitty.

Analyze the likely outcome of each lawsuit.

Liability of Corbin

> Was Hugs' loss reasonably foreseeable? — Hadley v. Baxendale
> 1st branch of test — likely not "ordinarily" foreseeable (address ambiguity in characterization)
> 2nd branch of test — Corbin not explicitly told about tickets or potential refund until after formation.
> But was informed that the castle was for millennium New Year's Eve fundraiser—ought to have known that tickets would be sold and may have to be refunded if party didn't take place.
> Were ticket-holders buying a right to attend any old party or a party in this castle with these turrets? Note that turrets were to be "highlight" of castle—suggests that they were essential to what ticket-holders bought.
> Even if reasonable to foresee economic loss, $5 million is an unusually large sum—may not have been foreseeable. Corbin wasn't told about price of tickets, but did know that it was (1) for a New Year's Eve party, (2) for the millennium, (3) in a castle and (4) for a fundraising event. All this suggests tickets would be expensive.
> Hugs' subsequent communication is irrelevant as it was after formation.

Liability of Chitty

> If Corbin is liable to Hugs, is Chitty liable to Corbin?
> 1st branch of test — same as above
> 2nd branch of test — Chitty was told far less than Corbin was— party could have been for a number of purposes. The word "crucial" doesn't communicate possibility of economic loss, certainly not of this magnitude.
> But what about the word "crucial" in context of 20 percent premium? Does premium reflect an assumption of risk by Chitty? Or simply additional costs associated with a rush job?

Andie's Answer for The Philosopher

1. The liability of Corbin and Chitty requires us to apply the <u>Hadley v. Baxendale</u> rule for determining liability for consequential loss. This rule is formulated as a two-part test under which we first ask whether the loss in question would arise in the ordinary course of things and, if not, whether the plaintiff communicated the prospect of the loss to the defendant. The overarching question is whether the loss in question was within the reasonable contemplation of the parties at the time of formation.

Liability of Corbin

A. Would This Loss Arise in the Ordinary Course of Things?

2. One should first note that there are difficulties of characterization attendant upon the determination of this question. The type of loss that might arise in "the usual course" is dependent upon how one describes this contract. Was this just a general commercial construction contract? Was it a contract for the construction of a castle? Or was it a contract for a castle with specific features to be constructed by a specific date? Our description of the kind of loss that might be expected in "the usual course" will vary in each of these cases.

3. One must resist the temptation to characterize the contract too specifically since this does violence to the concept "ordinary course of things". In other words, where the contract is characterized so specifically as to be one of a kind, it is difficult to even make sense of terms like "ordinary" or "usual".

4. Notwithstanding this, it would be inappropriate to choose a characterization as imprecise as "general commercial construction contract" since this fails to capture the essence of this transaction. In my judgment, this contract is most aptly characterized as one for the construction of a castle with particular features by a particular date. On its face, even this fairly specific characterization does not contemplate the kind of loss that occurred in this case. Therefore, it is necessary to proceed to the second branch of the <u>Hadley</u> v. <u>Baxendale</u> analysis.

B. Did The Communication Of Special Circumstances Bring This Loss Within The Reasonable Contemplation Of The Parties At The Time Of Formation?

5. At the time of formation, Corbin was informed that the castle was being built for a millennium New Year's Eve fundraiser. In these circumstances, was it reasonable for Corbin to know that failure to complete the castle on time would lead to Hugs having to refund the ticket-holders?

6. On the one hand, Corbin was not explicitly told at the time of formation that ticket-holders had a right to a refund, or even that tickets were being sold. This suggests that this type of loss was not a reasonably foreseeable consequence of failure to complete the castle.

7. On the other hand, it is arguable that this sort of loss should have been in Corbin's contemplation given the information that was in fact communicated to it. In other words, knowing the purpose for which the castle was being built, Corbin ought to have anticipated that tickets would be sold. Furthermore, Corbin arguably ought to have known that ticket-holders would be entitled to a refund if they did not receive what they paid for.

8. This raises the question of what it was reasonable for Corbin to think that the ticket-holders paid for. Again, there are problems of characterization here. Did they purchase the right to attend: (a) just any old party; (b) a party in a castle of no particular description; or, (c) a party in <u>this</u> particular castle with <u>these</u> particular turrets?

9. At first glance, it may appear odd that ticket-holders would be entitled to a refund simply because Hugs failed to provide them with a castle with turrets. However, Corbin ought to have known from the design plans that the turrets were to be the "highlight" of the castle. Thus, Corbin should have inferred that turrets were an essential part of what the ticket-holders contracted for. On balance, then, it looks as though Corbin ought to have known that what ticket-holders purchased was a right to attend a party at this particular castle with these particular turrets, and that they would be refunded their money if this was not provided them.

10. Taking all this into account, Hugs' failure to expressly inform Corbin of this potential loss would likely be of little significance. On this analysis, this type

of loss was reasonably foreseeable and Corbin would be liable for it under the <u>Hadley</u> v. <u>Baxendale</u> rule.

11. Granting that the <u>type</u> of loss suffered by Hugs was reasonably foreseeable, there may still be a further question as to whether the <u>extent</u> of that loss was so great as to render it unforeseeable. After all, $5 million (that is, 500 tickets at $10,000 each) is an unusually large sum to refund for a failed party. It is quite conceivable that Corbin could be liable to Hugs for some lesser (foreseeable) amount. Here again we must examine this question in the light of the <u>Hadley</u> v. <u>Baxendale</u> rule.

C. Was The Full Extent Of The Loss So Great As To Take It Out Of The Class Of Foreseeable Loss?

12. Corbin was never expressly told that the tickets were unusually expensive, let alone that they were worth $10,000 each. Thus, there is no sense in which the extent of this loss was expressly communicated to it.

13. Nevertheless, once again Corbin was provided with several pieces of information that arguably made it reasonable for it to think that the tickets would be unusually expensive. First, tickets to New Year's Eve parties are typically expensive, as compared to tickets for other events. The fact that this party was for the <u>Millennium</u> (a once in a lifetime event), and that it was being held in a castle being specially made for the occasion, should have suggested to Corbin that tickets to this party would be particularly expensive. Finally, Corbin knew that the party was a fundraiser. Tickets to these kinds of events are commonly very costly since the customers are not only purchasing the service but are also supporting a worthy cause.

14. Still, it is still difficult to imagine that tickets, even to such an exclusive event, would run $10,000 apiece. So, while Corbin is liable to Hugs for some portion of Hugs' consequential loss, it is unlikely that Corbin's liability extends to the full amount of Hugs' loss.

15. It is worth noting that Hugs' subsequent communication to Corbin regarding the cost of the tickets is of no relevance. Under the test in <u>Hadley</u> v. <u>Baxendale</u>, the determination of foreseeability is to be made at the time of formation. This, of course, is an instance of the general contract principle that

rights are determined as between the parties *inter se* at the time of formation.

Liability of Chitty

16. Given that Corbin is likely liable to Hugs for some of the cost of refunding the tickets, the question of whether Chitty is in turn liable to Corbin for this amount arises. Again, we must apply the <u>Hadley</u> v. <u>Baxendale</u> rule.

A. Would This Loss Arise In The Ordinary Course of Things?

17. Again, there are problems in characterizing the contract at issue. The same considerations that arose in relation to the contract between Hugs and Corbin apply here. I will not repeat them. Suffice it to say that, in my view, this contract is best characterized as one for the construction of turrets by a particular date. Once more, nothing in this is suggestive of the type of loss in question. This being the case, we must turn to the second branch of the <u>Hadley</u> v. <u>Baxendale</u> test.

B. Did the Communication of Special circumstances bring this loss within the reasonable contemplation of the parties at the time of formation?

18. Unlike Corbin, Chitty had very little knowledge about the specific nature of the party. It does not seem reasonable to impute to Chitty knowledge that tickets were being sold—for all Chitty knew the castle was being built for a party thrown by some eccentric millionaire. Use of the word "crucial", when combined with Chitty's knowledge that the turrets were "needed for a New Year's Eve party", arguably suggests that Chitty ought to have known that late performance would be a problem. But the word "crucial" says nothing about monetary loss, let alone loss in the amount of $5 million.

19. Of course, it may yet be the case that use of the word "crucial", when viewed in light of other features of the transaction, reasonably suggested to Chitty that such a loss was possible. After all, Chitty charged a 20 percent premium in response to Corbin's statement. It is possible that this entailed an assumption of responsibility by Chitty for any losses that Corbin might suffer as a result of tardiness.

20. On the other hand, the premium may have simply reflected the increased costs Chitty would need to incur to provide turrets on such short notice (for example, paying workers overtime to complete the project on time). Indeed, Chitty explicitly referred to Corbin's "time constraints," and not its potential financial loss, in setting its premium. On balance, then, the agreement between the parties would not seem to give rise to an objective expectation that Chitty was accepting responsibility for Corbin's consequential loss. Put more sharply, it is doubtful that this series of exchanges between the parties would tend toward the conclusion that Chitty is liable for that loss.

Post-Game Analysis

We will now break down Andie's answer with two objectives in mind. First we want to discuss how Andie's answer reflects her exam-writing strategy as well as the system she implemented throughout the semester. Second we want to suggest some ways in which Andie's answer might differ if she were writing for a professor other than The Philosopher.

Notice that Andie's answer is divided by subheadings that correspond to her outline. This is a basic but effective way to impose structural discipline on her answer. Also notice that Andie clearly sets out the problem very early in her answer (at paragraph 1).

A. Liability of Corbin

In Paragraphs 2 to 4 Andie acknowledges and addresses the ambiguity surrounding the application of the *Hadley* v. *Baxendale* test. We have seen how Andie's conversations with her friends, earlier in the term, brought out this ambiguity. The discussion they had at that time allowed Andie to easily deal with this issue on the exam.

In paragraphs 6 to 9 Andie is Tiger Spotting. She is playing with facts and trying to create two different characterizations based on the given facts. This reflects the emphasis Andie places on ambiguity in handling a fact pattern. Earlier in this chapter we discussed how IDAR should be implemented for different types of professors. What is common to all professors is their concern with ambiguity.

Accordingly, a discussion of ambiguity forms the heart of Andie's answer.

Note how in paragraph 9 Andie uses the fact that the turrets were to be the "highlight" of the castle to support a particular characterization. This fact came from the section of the fact pattern dealing with the contract between Corbin and Chitty, but here Andie is using this fact to analyze the contract between Corbin and Hugs. Reading the fact pattern twice facilitates this sort of "cross-pollination" of facts.

In paragraph 11 we see Andie discussing the extent of the loss as a distinct issue. When Andie was studying with her group we saw how this was one of the issues that came up. Having already considered this issue, it is easy for Andie to recognize it and address it on the exam. This is an example of how Tiger Spotting can pay dividends by allowing Andie to anticipate issues that might arise on the exam.

In paragraphs 12 and 13 Andy is Tiger Spotting again, this time with respect to the new issue raised in paragraph 11. What is noteworthy here is how Andie makes use of as many of the facts as she can. She assumes that every word in a fact pattern is there for a reason. This may turn out on inspection to be incorrect, but as a rule, this assumption prevents Andie from overlooking useful facts. Often, approaching the fact pattern in this way allows Andie to make creative use of the facts in ways that even the professor did not anticipate.

If Andie were writing for The Economist she might have reached a different conclusion regarding the extent of Corbin's liability than she did in paragraph 14 of the sample answer. In addition to (perhaps even as part of) her discussion of what loss was reasonably foreseeable, Andie would consider which decision would produce the optimal set of incentives for future contracting parties. For example, Andie would want to consider any informational asymmetries that might exist between the parties. She would want to point out how a given holding would affect the incentives faced by others, and she would want to question whether or not the test of reasonable foreseeability balanced the incentives in a way that led to an efficient result. Arguably, denying Hugs recovery of its consequential loss would create an incentive for parties in Hugs' position to reveal more information. Whether or not this would lead to more efficient bargains would depend on whether the benefits of additional information are outweighed by the increased transaction costs attendant on such disclosure.

In paragraph 15 Andie shows the professor that she recognizes the irrelevance of the communication made subsequent to formation of the contract. In doing so, Andie is keenly aware that she is writing for The Philosopher, for whom this fact constitutes a red herring. The lesson to be learned here is that such facts should not simply be disregarded. Often one can communicate one's understanding of the course not only by recognizing what is important but also by highlighting what is unimportant. If she were writing for The Politician, Andie might well have made different use of this fact. She might have argued that it would be inequitable to allow Corbin to knowingly cause loss to a charitable enterprise such as this one. As a society, we cannot tolerate behaviour that knowingly undermines support for disadvantaged individuals like law professors, who have given up lucrative downtown jobs for a life of selfless truth seeking.

Hugs's subsequent communication might also be worth discussing for The Economist. Indeed, this is an instance in which Andie might employ her strategy of raising an argument solely for the purposes of defeating it. Accordingly, she might suggest that at first blush the economic goal of encouraging disclosure of information would seem to be satisfied even by a subsequent communication. However, Andie might then observe that the fact that this disclosure was subsequent to formation is critical from an economic perspective. The reason we want information to be disclosed is to promote more efficient bargains. Thus, where information is disclosed when bargaining has been concluded, the objective of disclosure vis-à-vis bargaining has not been met.

B. Liability of Chitty

The first thing to note about this section of Andie's answer is how she frames the issue in paragraph 16. She connects Chitty's liability to Corbin's liability. This allows her to make a nice transition from the first section to the second while showing her professor that she is alive to the fact that the two issues, though distinct, are interrelated. She does not spend much time on this since it is a tangential matter that need only be nodded to. If Andie had determined that Corbin was not liable to Hugs, Andie would still address the question of

Chitty's liability. In that case, she would make it clear that she was addressing this question as an alternative answer. Andie knows that she should only preclude discussion of an issue where it is clear that the professor does not want her to address it.

In paragraphs 18 to 20 Andie has her Tiger-Spotting hat on once again. She uses every fact that she can—playing with the word "crucial", discussing the significance of the premium, and considering Chitty's referral to Corbin's "time constraints". These sorts of details are especially important in an exam written for Doctor Doctrine. If any of these details are similar to those contained in cases studied in the course, Andie will ensure that she draws an appropriate comparison. Doctor Doctrine is particularly appreciative of such comparisons where the cases referenced are obscure.

Take It to the BANK: Big Bills for FACT PATTERNS

- $ Don't treat exams as mechanical "tests" of what you've done before— continue to be strategic.
- $ Don't start writing too soon—let your thoughts percolate.
- $ Read the fact pattern twice and focus on different things each time.
- $ Make an outline—a structured answer is always a better one.
- $ Milk the facts—assume every fact is there for a reason.
- $ Tiger Spot—always be on the lookout for ambiguity.
- $ Keep your professor's preferred theory in mind—take every opportunity to show you understand it.
- $ Know which elements of IDAR to emphasize.
- $ Don't ignore red herrings—show that you see them for what they are.
- $ Don't assume you've arrived at the right answer and end things there—always address alternative arguments.

If Andie were writing for The Politician she might emphasize the fact that Chitty is a much smaller company than Corbin and is thus vulnerable and in need of legal protection. This fact might also be relevant for The Economist, not so much because of the smaller company's vulnerability but because larger companies are typically more sophisticated. Given this, the larger company is likely to be better placed to know which information needs to be disclosed.

For The Economist, Andie might also consider the fact that Chitty stood to gain an additional $10,000 by breaching its contract with Corbin. Andie might discuss this fact with reference to the concept of efficient breach. This concept holds that parties should be encouraged to breach if, and only if, doing so would maximize net aggregate wealth. In this instance, Chitty's breach appears to be efficient from its own one-sided perspective. However, we know Chitty's additional $10,000 gain is more than offset by Hugs' $5 million loss. Thus, what appears from Chitty's perspective to be an efficient breach only appears that way because of an information asymmetry. In other words, it was impossible for Chitty to know that its breach was inefficient. In this sense, the concept of efficient breach underscores the need for adequate disclosure.

Policy Questions

The focus of this chapter has been on how to approach fact pattern questions. This is appropriate since fact patterns constitute the better part of law school exams. However, many exams have an additional component often referred to as the "policy question". This type of question invites the student to step back and critically comment on some of the doctrines presented in the course or to compare different theoretical approaches to the material. We would be remiss if we did not at least offer some advice on how to approach this task.

Billie tends to view the policy question as a bit of an afterthought. For him, this is not what the course was ultimately about. To the extent that the policy question invites a consideration of doctrine or cases, Billie will attempt to put the finishing touches on the picture of diligence he has been painting. He will trot out cases and doctrine and perhaps parrot what some commentator had to say about the cases. If the policy question explicitly calls for a critical evaluation,

Billie will regurgitate his professor's comments from class, which of course, he has transcribed and memorized. And what else could Billie be expected to do? If the fact patterns appeared new and foreign to Billie, the policy question is bound to seem out of left field. Having spent all his time committing details to memory, Billie is not at all well placed to step back and analyze the course at a more abstract level.

Charlie welcomes policy questions. He knows they are the harbinger of the end of the exam. Just another forty minutes or so and he can head to the pub to commiserate with Carrie and Cass. Charlie is also typically less nervous when answering the policy question than when answering the fact patterns because he believes that his lack of knowledge of the material will be less apparent here. After all, he assumes that he can make vaguely critical comments about the course using highfalutin language as well as the next guy. If Billie's shortcoming is his inability to generate ideas, Charlie's problem is that he assumes that any idea will do.

Unlike her less evolved counterparts, Andie does not see the policy question as a pointless exercise in pseudo-philosophy or regurgitation. She recognizes that policy questions are a unique opportunity to convey a deeper understanding of the course without the constraints imposed by a fact pattern. This plays to Andie's strengths since much of her effort throughout the semester was directed at developing such an understanding.

In the policy question Andie finds that having played The Association Game and practised Story Telling really pays off. Both these exercises helped Andie synthesize the course into a unified whole. Because Andie has focused her efforts on gaining an understanding of her professor's theory, she is prepared to engage in an intelligent discussion of it. Additionally, she has studied particular doctrines and cases with this theory in mind, thereby enabling her to draw on examples from the course material to flesh out her theoretical discussion. And just as Andie's study techniques allowed her to anticipate the sort of ambiguities that her professor was likely to raise in a fact pattern, these techniques similarly helped her to anticipate the issues that the policy question seeks to address.

five

Paper Courses

FOR first-year law students, the primary method of evaluation consists of final exams that account for most—often all—of the course grade. A significant change in second and third year is that students have the option of taking courses in which they write papers rather than exams. In the next chapter, we will discuss considerations that are relevant to course selection generally. At this point, however, we assume that the decision has been made to take a paper course, and our aim is to outline a successful strategy given that decision. Not surprisingly, many of the skills developed in previous chapters will be relevant here. Still, it is necessary to acknowledge that paper courses are different. An appropriate strategy must take account of these differences.

Class Attendance and Reading

The most obvious difference between paper and exam courses is the classroom dynamic. Most paper courses are seminars with a greater emphasis on class participation. In part, this is due to the fact that seminars consist of fewer students and, in this more intimate environment, student participation is both invited and expected. Nonetheless, Charlie and Billie seem oblivious to this difference. As in exam classes, Charlie can be expected to be dozing off while Billie is likely to be scribbling madly. This leaves them ill suited to participate in class discussion. Andie is the only one who appears to be doing something different. She is listening intently but doing little in the way of note-taking. This means that Andie is well placed to exploit opportunities to participate in class.

In order to properly understand Andie's conduct in this regard, let us compare it to Billie's. The following syllogism brings to light the error of Billie's ways:

Major Premise: Note-taking is hard work and should only be done to the extent that it is of benefit.

Minor Premise: Note-taking is of little benefit in seminar courses.

Conclusion: Note-taking should be kept to a minimum in seminar courses.

Andie's law school experience establishes the soundness of this syllogism (as we will presently discover), yet if one walks into a law school seminar class there is no shortage of pens wagging in a senseless attempt to document the professor's every word. Billie's conduct in this regard is not only useless but ultimately counter productive.

After all, his apparent desire to be the professor's self-appointed scribe undermines Billie's ability to engage with what is going on in class. What Billie fails to realize is that his entire grade in a paper course rests on his thoughts on a subject that will usually be of his own choosing. Even where the professor assigns the topic there will be enough latitude for Billie to focus on those aspects of the topic with which he is most comfortable. Because he ultimately controls what his paper will be about, Billie need not—indeed cannot—rely on the professor to spoon-feed him valuable insights. Billie would be better served, in terms of positioning himself to write his paper, by setting down his pen and taking part in class discussion. This would enable him to test and refine his own ideas in an active dialogue with his professor and his peers.

This in fact is what Andie does. While Billie is mindlessly taking shorthand, Andie listens to and mulls over what is being said. She knows there is no point in documenting the details of the class discussion in her notes. Primarily, this is due to the fact that the breadth of material discussed in paper courses far outreaches what one could adequately treat in a single paper. In other words, the mode of evaluation downplays the importance of detailed knowledge of the entire course. Nor is it even necessary to have detailed knowledge of any particular section of the course. Instead, the mode of evaluation emphasizes the importance of a big-picture view.

Accordingly, Andie spends her classroom time trying to develop this big-picture view. In essence, this means working hard to ferret out her professor's preferred theory of the law as well as developing her own. As we have seen, theory is also important in an exam course, but only because it operates below the surface to help structure the way Andie handles the details of the cases and doctrines. One simply cannot deal with a fact pattern question without a solid understanding of these details. The role of theory is to help cement this understanding. Paper courses, in contrast, are more like policy questions: theory and synthesis come to the surface and the details are submerged.

Because of this, Andie does some of her deepest thinking in class. This allows her to formulate useful insights on the spot, which in turn allows her to actively engage in class discussion. And since the goal is to continuously synthesize the topics discussed in class with an eye toward ultimately implementing her synthetic understanding in the paper she writes, Andie is particularly involved in those elements of class discussion touching on topics that relate to her paper topic in some way.

This is not to suggest that Andie tunes out when the topic is not obviously related to her paper. For all sorts of reasons why Andie does her best to remain engaged in class discussion at all times. For one thing, it is often difficult to know in advance which topics will have some bearing on her paper. Indeed, given the emphasis Andie places on synthesis, she often finds that seemingly disconnected topics can yield extremely valuable insights in connection with her paper. For another, Andie quite likely has genuine academic interest in the topics that get discussed in class. Indeed, as we will see in the next chapter, that was one of Andie's principal motivations for choosing this course. Finally, there is a more base incentive for participating in class discussion in seminar courses: they often include a grade for class participation.

If Billie's classroom behaviour fails to take account of the difference between paper and exam courses, his approach to reading suffers even more obviously from the same defect. In a paper course, Billie reads every word that has been assigned, refusing to discriminate between the readings. In other words, he does exactly what he does in an exam class. Consequently, his experience is doomed to be exactly the same as it is in an exam class: he will be overworked and undercompensated for his efforts.

Andie, meanwhile, spends little time reading the assigned materials. In this sense, her behaviour in a paper course may, like Billie's, appear similar to her behaviour in an exam course. However, the impetus for this behaviour is quite different. In an exam course Andie knows that she must eventually acquire the details of the material from some source and will therefore only forego reading cases to the extent that she can find a suitable substitute. However, in a paper course Andie may never have use for these details (for reasons we have already discussed) and thus it may be possible for her to disregard certain readings altogether.

The corollary of this is that Andie will be sure to read any material for which she thinks she may have some use. Primarily, this means that she will read material that relates to her paper topic. If she has not yet formed a topic, she may read different articles in order to get a better sense of what she may wish to write on. In either case, Andie's purpose in reading will be to think about the ideas and arguments put forward and how she can make use of them in her paper.

Andie may also be motivated to read in order to be better prepared to participate in class discussion. Notice, however, that this only requires her to give the assigned readings a quick skim before class. Andie knows that she can get away with this because most professors spend a good chunk of class time summarizing and explaining the main ideas in the assigned readings. Moreover, the professor's exegesis will bring out what he views as the most important aspects of the readings. This information will be useful to Andie in the event that she later decides to read some of the material in greater detail.

Finally, Andie may also elect to read where she has an interest in the material quite apart from any concern over whether it is directly related to her paper topic. Of course, where this is true, Andie's reading will have less of the character of schoolwork and more of the character of pure enjoyment.

Selecting a TOPIC and APPROACH for the PAPER

If one thing can be said about the law school environment, it is that there is no shortage of whining. It is all too common to hear Charlie (or sometimes even Billie) say, "I wrote a great paper for The Philosopher. It disagreed with his theory, but man it was tight! Somehow I still got a C+. Where's the justice?" Of course, the justice for which Charlie is pining would be more appropriate to a utopian world than to the real world. In the real world, professors, like the rest of us, cannot help but filter the arguments they encounter through their own subjective experience of things. Thus, however pleasant-sounding and appealing the utopian vision may seem, it must inevitably be exposed as naively idealistic.

"My professor thinks he's got it all figured out, but I think he's got it all wrong. This masterpiece is going to blow him away!"

To be sure, law schools, like most academic environments, attract a diversity of views. Most law school administrations see that as part of their mandate. That said, one cannot write whatever one wants on any subject of one's choosing and receive a good grade on the strength of literary skill alone. Anyone who wishes to do well on a law school paper must take account of the person for whom she is writing. Billie and Charlie fail to recognize this, so when they produce what they consider to be masterpieces that are not validated (with good grades), they complain of professorial prejudice.

To Charlie, catering to such "prejudice" would essentially amount to "selling out." Since he gave up on doing well long ago, Charlie expresses his disillusionment (or, as he prefers to call it, his "enlightenment") through taking what he sees to be the high road, challenging established norms by disagreeing with everything his professor has said in class. This approach makes sense given Charlie's psychological profile. Having eschewed academic success as base and mundane, he seeks confirmation of his worth from a source other than his transcript. And, at any rate, he is more than happy to give himself a ready-made excuse for the bad grade he is certain that he will receive. It should come as no surprise that Charlie's expectations are not disappointed—his sense of spiritual superiority comes at the cost of martyrdom in the form of a bad grade.

Billie, meanwhile, does not immediately register what he later condemns as professorial prejudice. At first, he is essentially oblivious to who is teaching the class. Because he has been too busy documenting and reading, he has missed out on many of the essential aspects of the course. In particular, he does not have a terribly good sense of his audience. Although Billie does not consciously sabotage himself as Charlie does, he puts all his faith in brute effort (and perhaps his research skills). If he has chosen a professor who appreciates these qualities, Billie is in luck. More often, however, he finds himself having spent a great deal of time and effort writing his paper, with less than satisfying results.

Unlike her two counterparts, Andie recognizes that one person's prejudice is another's considered judgment. As we mentioned in chapter 1, professors have typically spent years thinking about and developing their views, with the result that the theories they favour are, as they see it, supported by the balance of argument. Andie ensures that she is properly respectful of this fact in every aspect of her paper-writing strategy. She chooses a paper topic that engages with the professor's preferred theory rather than one that merely reflects her own interests. She makes certain that she speaks his language rather than supplanting it with her own. She takes pains to get inside his theoretical framework in an effort to understand it, rather than launching external criticisms of it. And, perhaps most importantly, she runs arguments that she knows he will be receptive to rather than ones that will offend his intellectual sensibilities.

If Andie has been wise (and she usually is), none of this need entail selling out. As we will see in the next chapter, Andie has the deck stacked in her favour before she even begins to think about choosing a topic. In her view, if engaging with a professor's theoretical approach is so disagreeable as to constitute selling out, she is better off never enrolling in his class to begin with than she is trying to butt heads with him. Indeed, Andie does her best to ensure that she enrolls in courses taught by professors who happen to share her own preferred theoretical slant. Of course, if she somehow finds herself stuck in a class with the wrong kind of professor, Andie will inevitably bite the bullet and play his game. For, Andie never loses sight of her ultimate goal, which is not intellectual vindication, but academic success. At any rate, if she really cares to challenge one of her professor's views, she can always publish her intellectual manifesto on the Internet.

Researching the PAPER

Among the biggest shoes that get kicked around the legal community is that there is a necessary correlation between one's familiarity with the law library, and one's academic success. It is not unusual to hear a practising lawyer react to the knowledge that one is a law student by exclaiming: "You must be spending a ton of time at the library!" He may even suggest that this establishes a bond of kinship between you: "My practice consists of blah, blah, blah, which requires me to spend a lot of time doing research. Not much different from law school, really." Those who espouse such views are no doubt trying to make sense of and validate their own experiences as law students. Indeed, many lawyers and law students alike seem to take pride in the volume of research they do. It is as though they picture themselves as the legal equivalents of Sherlock Holmes, burning the midnight oil in investigative pursuit of that elusive judgment, hiding in some dark corner of the globe, which establishes the argument they need to prove. There is something tragically comical in seeing them, chests puffed out to the point of popping the buttons on their shirts, as they boast, "You know, there's a lower court judge in Singapore who, in an unreported decision (I can't actually tell you how I got my hands on it, but trust me, it was tough), made the same argument that I just gave you."

This caricature, incredible as it may seem, essentially captures Billie's approach to trying to produce a successful law school paper. Billie spends countless hours looking for that one case, eagerly gathering reams of paper and racking up countless hours on online research databases. He reads an enormous volume of material—both cases and secondary sources — to ensure that he leaves no doctrinal stone unturned. He begins his research early in the semester, perhaps as early as the first day of class, in order to ensure that he has time to do all this. And indeed, when his paper is finally written, it will be riddled with footnotes, reflecting his prodigious research skill and the breadth of knowledge on the subject that it has produced.

Charlie reacts to Billie's efforts with a kind of grudging admiration. On the one hand, he cannot help but be impressed by the mountain of research Billie has managed to compile. On the other hand, he has little inclination to climb this mountain himself. The effort required would be too great. So Charlie avoids research until fear of an impending deadline sets in. At that point, he hits the library stacks in a panic-stricken attempt to imitate Billie's effort. Unfortunately for Charlie, by then it is too late. He typically finds that others have already signed out the best books on his subject. As a result, Charlie's paper leaves his professor wondering why he has ignored the leading authorities. As for any materials Charlie does find, because he does not have enough time to read them, he ends up either not using them at all or referring to them only tangentially. His effort to show that he has researched and understood a vast quantity of material therefore fails. Instead, he appears to be a scattered and shallow thinker.

Charlie's mistake is not necessarily that he spends insufficient time researching his paper (though he may spend insufficient time on his paper more generally). It is that he thinks that the secret to successful paper writing lies in imitating Billie. This leaves him doomed from the outset: his efforts will inevitably appear to the professor to be nothing more than a cheap copy of Billie's. In any contest between a stronger and a weaker implementation of the same strategy, the former is bound to win out.

However, this should not be taken to be a vindication of Billie's approach to paper writing. Charlie's avoidance of heavy research is entirely understandable. There may be some who enjoy the detective work that is done in a library, but for many, thorough research is time-consuming and dreary.

The question, then, is what to do if one falls into the latter camp? Andie, for one, knows that there is neither cause for despair, nor for any attempt to morph — at great personal cost — into a carbon copy of Billie. For, unlike Billie and Charlie, Andie realizes that research can be minimized by implementing an integrated strategy that begins with choosing her courses correctly and continues with knowing her audience (the professor) and the type of treatment he expects a paper topic to be given.

No doubt a 40-page paper that contains 150 footnotes citing 70 cases and 30 secondary sources is likely to be well received by Doctor Doctrine. If, in addition to these qualities, the paper discusses the most recent cases and commentary from a number of common law jurisdictions, it may even be the case that it will be assured of receiving his highest commendation.

However, that very same paper—and it is the paper that Billie always produces—will, without more, garner considerably less appreciation from The Philosopher. Indeed, Billie is often amazed to find that his detailed research and extraordinary effort goes almost completely unnoticed by The Philosopher. Andie might well have predicted this outcome. She knows that The Philosopher is less concerned with how many sources can be cited in support of an argument than he is with considerations such as whether the argument is carefully explored, whether it advances the paper's theoretical objectives, and whether it provides insight into the nature of Law.

She also knows that, although The Philosopher wants to see arguments connected to case law, there is little to be gained by citing all the obscure cases that one might cite for Doctor Doctrine. The Philosopher is primarily interested in the leading cases and landmark judgments. There is, after all, a *reason* that they are the "leading" cases and "landmark" judgments: in The Philosopher's view, it is that they enunciate principles that are at the heart of Law, principles whose careful examination can therefore reveal a great deal about the immanent rationality of Law. Thus, rather than seeing references to obscure cases from faraway lands, The Philosopher would much prefer to see a careful and rigorous analysis of this handful of leading cases. Indeed, the colossal research effort that is appreciated by Doctor Doctrine may not only go unappreciated by The Philosopher, it may even be detrimental to one's grade. For him, an exploration of so many cases may be perceived as a failure to explore the important questions with the requisite level of depth.

Somewhere between the two poles of Doctor Doctrine and The Philosopher lie The Politician and The Economist. By recognizing this, Andie knows that she can calibrate the amount of effort she must put into research simply by making careful course selections, choosing courses taught by professors whose requirements with regard to research match her preferences.

We encourage the reader who is skeptical about these claims to spend some time in the library conducting the following experiment. Look at a few articles written by each of The Philosopher, The Economist, The Politician, and Doctor Doctrine. Then look at the number of footnotes in the paper and the number of sources cited. Because, other things being equal, a longer paper will obviously have more footnotes than a shorter paper, make a rough adjustment for their length. What the reader will find, generally speaking, is that the number of cases and secondary sources cited by these various professors can be ordered roughly in accordance with the amount of research that, in Andie's estimation, they require of their students. In other words, Doctor Doctrine will cite the greatest number of cases and sources; The Philosopher will cite the least; and The Politician and The Economist will be somewhere in the middle. (Incidentally, this exercise is useful, not merely for determining the quantity, but also the *types* of materials cited by the various professors.) One can safely assume that all these professors will expect no more, and no less, of a research effort in papers completed for them by students.

Take It to the BANK: Big Bills for PAPER COURSES

- $ Don't take detailed notes in class — it's the discussion that matters.
- $ Do assigned readings with your paper in mind — you definitely won't be examined on them.
- $ Write your paper with your audience in mind — apply his or her preferred approach rather than supplanting it with your own.
- $ Research is a matter of choice rather than necessity.

six

Selecting COURSES

It's the first day back from summer break. The law school cafeteria is buzzing with nervous energy and the sound of cheerful greetings. Refreshed, students are ready to embark on another semester of law school. The previous year's results are now unalterable history and Andie, Billie, and Charlie can look forward to a clean start, with new courses and new professors. The questions that face our three friends are "which courses?" and "which professors?"

We have seen how Andie approaches her classes, how she studies for and writes exams, and how she writes papers. With respect to these activities, Andie has a dominant strategy over Billie and Charlie. The dominance of Andie's strategy doesn't end there: it extends to every facet of the law school experience, including planning the semester. To see how this is so, consider the kinds of considerations that go into planning the semester of her two foils.

Charlie: Hey Billie, good to see ya. How'd last semester go?

Billie: All right I suppose. Thought I might have done better in Trusts. I knew that course cold and filled five booklets on the exam. Must have missed something. Anyway, do you have your courses sorted out yet?

Charlie: Yep. My buddy just got a new snowmobile up at his cottage so I fixed it so that I don't have any classes on Friday and Monday. I don't know anyone in my classes and my exam schedule is brutal, but I'll worry about that when the time comes.

Billie: My schedule is not the greatest either, but I know I want to practise corporate law so I didn't have much choice. Also, The Politician told me I really should take Admin Law.

While this exchange illustrates that Billie and Charlie do put some thought into their course selection, it is apparent that the one consideration that does not enter into their thought process is academic success. Charlie, having long ago foregone any hopes of achieving academic success, manipulates his schedule to accord him the maximum amount of social benefit. Billie chooses his courses the way he approaches them. He puts his head down and plows forward, refusing to let strategic thinking deter him from doing what he believes must be done.

Andie knows that scheduling classes can have a significant impact on her grades and her quality of life. As with other law school decisions, a little forethought can make things easier and more enjoyable, but only if one is considering and evaluating relevant criteria.

Andie's Criteria for PICKING COURSES

Because Andie has a system, or a set of basic principles that help her maneuver through the obstacle course that is law school, she is able to identify and weigh the myriad factors that should go into deciding the academic content and structure of the semester. In a nutshell, Andie chooses courses that allow her to implement and take advantage of the ideas and methods that comprise her system. She is attuned to the type of professor who is teaching each course. She knows the importance of collaborative learning and is aware that she will not be able to reap its benefits if she takes classes full of individuals whose company she does not enjoy. She is cognizant of the time commitments involved in writing a good paper as opposed to preparing for an exam. She is well aware that one's success at any task is typically proportionate to the enthusiasm and enjoyment one can generate in relation to that task. And, finally, she knows that the received wisdom on how one should pick courses can sometimes be misleading.

Recall Billie's comment to Charlie regarding the advice he

received from The Politician. The Politician, with the best of intentions, proclaimed that because of the ubiquitous nature of administrative law, Billie would be doing himself a disservice by not taking that class. This kind of advice is typical of the received wisdom at law school. Billie, being the sort who prides himself on doing what must be done, always takes such advice as gospel. As a result, at the end of his law school career Billie will be able to look at himself in the mirror with the pride attendant on knowing that he has acquired a "complete legal education". Unfortunately, this sense of pride comes at considerable cost. Billie's religious adherence to received gospel will leave him understimulated, overworked, and facing a brutal exam schedule. To make matters worse, Billie will face this semester-long ordeal without the benefit of companionship or assistance from others who might have made the road a little easier to travel. What is *most* complete about Billie's legal education, then, is the sense of despair it will engender in him.

Indeed, because Andie questions received wisdom, she quickly discovers that this may be the *only* way in which Billie's education is "complete". The value that Billie places on completeness has two aspects. The first is instrumental: he worries that without taking all the "core" courses he will be ill prepared for both the bar exams and the practice of law. The second is pedagogical: he thinks that there is a defined body of legal knowledge that anyone must master in order to be deserving of a law school diploma. In Andie's view, both of these perceptions are misguided.

In the first instance, Andie knows that neither the bar exams nor the practice of law will depend on taking any given course. There are, in fact, courses specifically designed to prepare one for bar exams. As for practice, Andie sees no reason why she cannot acquire virtually all of what she needs to know on the fly. Indeed, Andie has friends practising at prestigious law firms who can confirm this for her anecdotally. They tell her that the solutions to most legal problems, whether in the field of administrative law or in any other field, are easily ascertainable without having studied the particular area of law at issue. At most, they indicate, taking a given course will save one the hour or so that it takes to get oriented with the material, but saving this one hour of time hardly justifies sacrificing grades and quality of life for an entire semester.

Nor are there strong pedagogical reasons for pursuing the

"complete" legal education. Andie knows that beyond the fundamental courses that make up the first-year curriculum — which even
she sees as the foundation of a legal education — there are few courses that everybody *must* take. Of course, Billie is likely to respond to
this claim incredulously: "Are you suggesting that the courses one
takes are irrelevant?" Charlie, on the other hand, may chime in
enthusiastically: "You've got that right: all these courses are useless!"
As usual, both miss the point entirely. Law school classes are neither
irrelevant nor useless. Andie's only claim is that no *one* course, or
even set of courses, is essential to a proper legal education.

The courses Andie takes help her, on the aggregate, to acquire an
understanding of Law — a conceptually integrated phenomenon that
permeates our lives. Throughout various areas of the law, the
same principles and considerations play themselves

> "Oh sure course X is tough — but
> believe you me, no legal education is
> complete without it!"

out. Of course, for pragmatic and pedagogical reasons, classes consist of artificially discrete topics of study.
But in reality, the content of any one course cannot be neatly segre-
gated from other areas of the law. When taking a class in Wills and
Estates, for example, one encounters principles relevant to Family
Law and Trusts. Thus, it is impossible to go through law school without developing a general idea of how Law works. Even Charlie will
glean some understanding of the interplay between statutes and case
law, the legislature and the judiciary, the state and the individual, *et
cetera*. If the details of a given area of law are a mystery, this can be
quickly remedied by spending a few hours consulting a textbook,
examining statutes, and perhaps reading a few of the leading cases.
Given this, the specific content of a course is a variable that should be
accorded little weight when calculating the pros and cons of various
scheduling possibilities. Since Andie appreciates this point, she has
greater flexibility in choosing her courses and is able to make choices
that facilitate painless academic success.

Picking Courses You Are Interested In

Academic interest is Andie's initial consideration when devising a potential schedule. At first blush this may not appear to be an impressive bill. The cynic will likely regard this advice as being on par with such priceless tidbits as "look both ways before you cross the street" and "buy low and sell high". The cynic, as is often the case, is correct. Like these two hackneyed examples, this advice is obvious, trite, and *extremely effective*. Just as looking both ways before you cross the street is an effective way to ensure you will not get run over, enrolling in courses you find interesting is an effective way to avoid being blindsided when grades are released. A class in which Andie is interested offers her the best of both worlds: it allows her to enjoy herself while increasing her chances of academic success.

Indeed, as we have stressed throughout, enjoyment and success are mutually propagating. The more Andie is interested in a course, the more time she will spend talking about it. Andie finds such conversation both entertaining and crucial to developing her understanding of the law, and as this understanding develops, Andie increases her chance of law school success.

Even if all this sounds obvious, what is less obvious, because few people stop to consider it, is how interest is generated in the first place. Most people equate interest with some inherent quality in the topic itself. Although there is something to this, in Andie's view, there are at least two other factors that come into play here. First, Andie recognizes that more than inherent interest, the manner in which a topic is presented and discussed will go a long way to determining her level of interest in it. As with all of us, Andie favours treatments that accord with her own preferred approach to law. Consequently, she takes courses with professors who share that approach. Second, and this falls directly out of the value she places on conversation, Andie knows that her interest in a course is enhanced by having friends take the course with her. After all, one needs others with whom to converse.

Selecting Classes as a Group

Picking classes with friends is arguably the most important factor in Andie's class selection equation. By now it should be apparent that Andie approaches law school as a joint enterprise. Group synergy is a non-interest-bearing, unlimited line of credit and Andie is not shy about withdrawing bills when needed. The best way to take advantage of this synergy is to schedule classes *as a group*. Scheduling her classes with the group also facilitates and greatly enhances Andie's enjoyment of the day-to-day routine of the semester. Sharing similar schedules with individuals whose company she enjoys makes it easy to get together for academic and social activities and, most important, those activities that are a hybrid of the two. Andie does not have to worry about when she can meet up with this or that person for lunch or try to remember when a certain individual has a class on Tuesday. She simply goes about her daily business knowing that her social and academic interactions have long since been arranged.

Given the obvious benefits of this strategy, why do Billie and Charlie seem to ignore it when considering which classes they should take? Not even Andie could have an answer to this question (with or without the benefit of consultation with her friends). Perhaps it is a belief in the fallacious notion that enjoyment and academic success are conflicting goals. Or maybe Billie and Charlie believe that taking classes with their friends is a practice that should have been outgrown in junior high. Whatever ostensible justification Billie and Charlie might offer, Andie wants none of it. Andie knows that enjoyment and academic success are not mutually exclusive, and she is not prepared to disregard an opportunity to attain both merely because choosing classes with friends *appears* juvenile.

Choosing The Right Professor

As stated, Andie knows that the manner in which course material is presented will greatly influence her interest in a course. In turn, the professor who is teaching a course will greatly affect the manner in which the material is presented. Consequently, the identity of the professor teaching a course largely determines whether Andie is likely to find it interesting.

Given this, how does Andie go about determining what different professors are like? After first year there are only a handful of professors with whom Andie will be personally acquainted. It is, of course, relatively easy to obtain information about other professors at her school, but it is somewhat more difficult to obtain information that is *properly informative*. Most of the wisdom concerning professors floated around law school is circulated by Billie and Charlie. The following typifies the sort of conversation that Billie and Charlie might be expected to have regarding a prospective instructor.

Charlie: Hey Billie, what do you know about Doctor Doctrine?

Billie: I know this much: you better sign up for his class right now or you'll be put on a waiting list! My friend Bobbie says he's awesome! He's a super-nice guy, he talks about *all* the cases, his exams are fair, and he wrote the book on Admin Law —*literally!*

Charlie: Yeah, I heard he's an easy grader too. Sign me up!

Billie and Charlie believe that if a professor is well liked by his students and a respected authority on some area of law he will necessarily be a good instructor *for them.* They take the question of how "good" a professor is to be an objective question, on which most students will necessarily agree. Accordingly, any consideration of the "fit" between a professor and themselves is conspicuously absent from their criteria for choosing courses.

In contrast, Andie does not ignore the distinction between a highly regarded professor and a professor who is good *for her.* She knows that a well-liked and widely respected professor may be a great choice, but for reasons that go beyond his reputation. To her, considerations regarding the professor's temperament, the volume of reading he assigns, or his pedigree, are of secondary concern. She is more concerned about the professor's approach to Law. As already suggested, Andie's interest in a course is directly related to the manner in which the material is presented. Thus, for Andie, a large part of choosing courses involves choosing professors whose thoughts interest her.

As we have seen, Andie has a preferred theoretical framework, which she uses to analyze legal problems and doctrine. This allows Andie to contemplate and discuss virtually any legal issue that may arise in a manner that is interesting to her and to others who share her preference for that theory of law. Because the *theory* is interesting and intellectually stimulating to Andie, any use of that theory to analyze legal problems cannot help but engender passion and interest in her. This is true even if—perhaps *especially* if—the analysis is largely devoted to criticizing the doctrine and cases arising from an area of law that holds no *inherent* interest for her.

What this means, of course, is that Andie is bound to be interested in courses taught by professors who share her preferred theory of law. Andie may well be able to engage with course material in an interesting manner in spite of the professor teaching the course—indeed she will always strive to do so—but signing up for a course that is being taught by a professor whose approach to law is unappealing to her is asking for trouble. This is true for two crucial reasons.

First, the professor's approach will be reflected both in class discussion of the material and in his initial choice of the material that will be covered. If his approach is completely uninspiring to Andie, it will be difficult for her to tolerate the hours she spends in class. At the limit, she may even be forced to opt for a strategy that entails foregoing class attendance altogether.

Second, the professor's theoretical framework helps Andie, in concert with her friends, to synthesize course material and thus develop a larger understanding of the subject. This larger understanding is what distinguishes her exam answers and her papers from those of Billie, whose brute knowledge is at least a match for her own. Where the professor's theoretical approach to law is unappealing to Andie, it will therefore be more difficult for her to distinguish herself. She must still attempt to do so, of course, but her relative lack of interest in his approach makes it less likely that she will develop the requisite level of understanding. A corollary of this is that if a professor's approach to law is not grounded in any theory at all, Andie is comparatively disadvantaged when writing an exam or a paper for him. This being the case, Andie will only take classes taught by Doctor

Doctrine where there are other competing, and overriding, interests at stake.

If Doctor Doctrine is at one end of the spectrum, a professor whose theory accords with Andie's own is at the other end. In his class, Andie's preferred theory is not just a way for her and her friends to understand the class: it *is* the class. Accordingly, class discussions will inevitably be engaging, entertaining, and educational. Moreover, the course material selected by the professor is bound to seem both interesting and illuminating to Andie: after all, an individual who shares Andie's perspective selected it.

As well as breeding enjoyment, sharing the professor's general approach is also highly conducive to achieving a good grade. It ensures that Andie's paper or exam will be read by a receptive audience. The connection between this and achieving a good grade should be obvious by now.

All of which raises the following question: How does one go about ascertaining the preferred theoretical approach of one's professors before even having taken their classes? To begin with, Andie is not shy about enrolling in classes with professors who have taught courses she has taken and enjoyed in the past. She can also seek the advice of these professors when she is searching for other classes to take. If, for example, Andie was enthralled with The Philosopher's approach to one of her first-year classes, she will be sure to ask him to recommend any upper-year classes taught by like-minded colleagues. Looking into a professor's academic background (including his most notable work) can also be helpful in determining how the professor is likely to approach the course he is teaching. Finally, if all else fails, Andie can turn to the grapevine, always being careful to weed out advice based on a professor's alleged sense of humour or his purported pedigree.

Considering the Mode of Evaluation

A more mundane criterion, which is nonetheless crucial, is the mode of evaluation. Two questions arise in connection with this criterion: (1) How will Andie be evaluated?; and (2) When will she have to do the work? Billie willfully disregards both questions. To be sure, he may end up with a mixture of paper and exam courses, but he is largely indifferent to the exact balance. Certainly he does not consider his mix of courses with the same nuanced attention to detail as Andie does. Billie may even have an aversion to selecting a course of studies based on how and when he will be evaluated, as he did with choosing classes with friends. For him, law school is a test of will. He would not be able to look at himself in the mirror if he let such base considerations inform the content of his studies. Indeed, he leaves such base considerations to Charlie and his ilk. Charlie, of course, is happy to entertain these considerations, if only because he has already booked his flight to Cancun and needs to ensure that his exam schedule accommodates this.

Like Charlie, Andie unabashedly chooses her classes with such mundane factors in mind. Unlike Charlie, she does so to the benefit of her academic and intellectual experience, not at its expense. At first blush, focusing on the method of evaluation may appear to ignore what many would consider the fundamental purpose of law school: learning. Andie knows that appearances can be deceiving. In fact, Andie's strategy—both in general, and in terms of course selection in particular—is designed to overcome two significant obstacles to learning: grade anxiety and a dearth of time. By scheduling classes in a strategic manner, Andie frees up the time and energy required to indulge in true academics, learning for the sake of learning as opposed to learning for the sake of a grade. More time in general means, among other things, more time for engaging with course material. As we have seen, this cannot help but be reflected in Andie's superior understanding of the material and, ultimately, in her grades as well. This should dispel any aversion to appealing to these kinds of mundane considerations in choosing one's courses. Let us now see, more specifically, how it is that these considerations factor into Andie's course selection equation.

How Is the Course Evaluated?

Classes are typically evaluated by one of the following methods: a 100 percent final exam; a 100 percent term paper; a series of short papers; or some combination thereof. Andie knows that she will be best served by choosing courses with modes of evaluation that play to her strengths. If exams are her forte she picks classes that allow her to take advantage of this fact; if she genuinely loves to write she is happy to pick a schedule that entails writing a number of papers.

Saying this, Andie's strengths are not to be evaluated in isolation from her participation in a study group. Put another way, her study group *is* one of Andie's strengths. Accordingly, her choice of mode of evaluation is respectful of this fact. For example, Andie will avoid taking exam classes without her core group. This is less true of paper courses. The reason for this lies in the nature of exams as compared to papers. As we have seen, exams emphasize the importance of course details, about which one's study group will have little to say if not taking the course. In contrast, basic theoretical concepts come to the fore in paper courses. Given that Andie and her friends share a preferred theoretical approach to law, her friends should therefore still have much to offer in the way of assistance in writing a paper for a course they are not taking.

When Must the Work Be Done?

Another factor that enters into Andie's contemplation when she is scheduling her classes concerns the distribution of her workload throughout the semester. To the extent that Andie can distribute her workload, so that she can concentrate on different courses at different points throughout the semester, this cannot help but improve both her lifestyle and her chances at academic success. This reflects the fact that the value of an hour fluctuates over time. Just as fresh fruit is worth a lot more in the winter than in the summer, an hour in December is far more valuable to a law student than an hour in September.

This idea plays out in each of the following ways. First, leaving aside any differences in the aggregate amount of time required to write a paper as compared with preparing for an exam, the time constraints imposed by these different modes of evaluation are of significant impact. Exam courses inevitably require Andie to undergo a relatively intense period of focus at the end of term, but may not take up as much of her time during the course of the semester. With a paper, Andie has greater flexibility in terms of scheduling her work. Indeed, Andie believes that the best way to write a paper is over a long period, giving the ideas with which she is working time to evolve and mature. To be sure, the exercise of actually getting the words down on a piece of paper may be done in a short, intense period of time, but even when this is true a great deal of thought will have necessarily taken place prior to this, rendering this last act merely a mechanical act of transcription. Because of this, Andie takes a mix of paper and exam courses, even though she may have a strong preference for one mode of evaluation over the other.

Andie may also take advantage of any opportunity to enroll in a course in which the work is due prior to the end of the semester. If she enrolls in a course that is evaluated throughout the semester (say by a series of small papers), and is completed by the time the exam period begins, she will have more time when it is needed most. Even supposing that a series of small papers results in an expenditure of more total time than an exam course, because the hours are spent when time is least valuable (that is, earlier in the semester), this may still represent a more efficient use of her time.

Finally, the fluctuating value of time is of particular importance during exam period itself. Andie is aware that preparation for an exam requires her to concentrate her efforts in the days immediately preceding the exam. All else being equal, Andie therefore avoids having to write exams that are not spaced several days apart. This is not to say that Andie cannot study for more than one exam at a time; it is simply meant to emphasize that doing so is less than optimal. Among the implications of this is that Andie will not take a

Take It to the BANK: Big Bills for COURSE SELECTION

- $ There is no such thing as a course you *must* take.
- $ Pick courses as a group.
- $ Pick courses you are intested in, recognizing the various ways in which interest is generated.
- $ A good professor is one who is good for you — pick classes with professors who share your preferred approach.

course that might otherwise be of great interest to her if it does not fit with the rest of her exam schedule. There is no unhappy compromise here: being systematic about law school means that interest is to be maximized on the whole, and not with respect to any single course considered in isolation.

It should never be forgotten, in connection with this, that one's sustained interest in a course of studies cannot be divorced from being able to maintain a balanced lifestyle. Thus, the final way in which this factor plays out in Andie's course selection criteria is to ensure that she will have plenty of time to spend with her friends at the local watering hole. No doubt, a great deal of that time will be taken up discussing, arguing, ruminating, and philosophizing on issues that are of academic importance. But squeezed in there somewhere will also be a healthy dose of playful banter on a variety of topics ranging from law school gossip to that episode where Bugs Bunny poses as a square dance leader and causes two hillbillies to thrash each other with fence posts.

Afterword

There is an issue that has been hanging over this book—or waiting in the weeds, if you prefer—almost from the very outset. Given that law students are graded against each other, the utility of any "how to" book on law school is likely to diminish over time in direct proportion to the success of the approach it outlines. For, as more students come to see the value in that approach, and therefore adopt it for themselves, each of them loses more of the relative advantage she had on others who had not yet cottoned on, as it were. We should say a few words about this issue by way of giving a few final pieces of advice.

In one sense, the sort of concern raised by this issue is of a piece with the very competitiveness—the fixation with the zero-sum nature of the law school grading system—from which we have consistently tried to steer the reader clear. Indeed, it was this sort of competitiveness that created the need for this book in the first place (at least in part). Ideally, we will have demonstrated with sufficient clarity the dangers of such competitiveness, so that the reader will be more likely to resist the temptation to make heavy weather of this issue.

Freed of this temptation, it is our view that the reader will come to see that the advice set out in this book continues to offer substantial benefit regardless of how many law students should come to read it. Its true benefits, in fact, are to be measured in absolute rather than relative terms. Put more sharply, while it is true that one's academic performance relative to other students will not improve if everyone reads this book (assuming, of course, that all students are equally adept at implementing the strategies it outlines), there are ways in which reading this book will help improve everyone's law school experience absolutely. These absolute benefits are both instrumental and intrinsic.

In the first instance, since our goal in this book has been to set out a system for achieving academic success with a minimum of effort, students will be better off for having read this book in terms of the time they free up for other pursuits. This instrumental benefit — the improvement to one's quality of life — continues to persist regardless of how many students are employing the same system.

In addition, this book has set out a system for ensuring that any time spent working, rather than engaging in these other pursuits, will be considerably more enjoyable. This too goes to quality of life. But in our view it is better understood as an intrinsic, rather than an instrumental, benefit. For while it is in the nature of a book like this to speak in instrumental terms (indeed, that is just what is entailed by offering advice on "how to" achieve a certain goal), it is our hope that somewhere along the line the reader has come to appreciate that enjoyment of the law school experience — in itself, and for its own sake — represents the most important and lasting benefit that one can acquire.

Virtually all students go to law school with some sort of nascent interest in law. At some point — most likely when the competitiveness starts — that interest typically begins to dwindle, inevitably to be replaced by frustration and disenchantment with the law school experience. If nothing else, we hope to leave the reader with renewed hope that law school *can* be interesting, that the study of this intellectually rich discipline *is* rewarding and enjoyable. Indeed, as we have stressed at other points throughout this book, enjoyment and interest are mutually propagating and reinforcing. If the reader can come to appreciate the importance of this point in connection with the study of law, she will walk away with the greatest benefit we could wish for any law student.

Appendix

Hadley v. Baxendale (1854), 9 Exch. 341, 156 Eng.Rep. 145. (Court of Exchequer)

... At the trial before Crompton, J., at the last Gloucester Assizes, it appeared that the plaintiffs carried on an extensive business as millers at Gloucester; and that on the 11th on May, their mill was stopped by a breakage of the crank shaft by which the mill was worked. The steam-engine was manufactured by Messrs. Joyce & Co., the engineers, at Greenwich, and it became necessary to send the shaft as a pattern for a new one to Greenwich. The fracture was discovered on the 12th, and on the 13th the plaintiffs sent one of their servants to the office of the defendants, who are the well-known carriers trading under the name of Pickford & Co., for the purpose of having the shaft carried to Greenwich. The plaintiffs' servant told the clerk that the mill was stopped, and that the shaft must be sent immediately; and in answer to the inquiry when the shaft would be taken, the answer was, that if it was sent up by twelve o'clock any day, it would be delivered at Greenwich on the following day. On the following day the shaft was taken by the defendants, before noon, for the purpose of being conveyed to Greenwich, and the sum of 2l. 4s. was paid for its carriage for the whole distance; at the same time the defendants' clerk was told that a special entry, if required, should be made to hasten its delivery. The delivery of the shaft at Greenwich was delayed by some neglect; and the consequence was, that the plaintiffs did not receive the new shaft for several days after they would otherwise have done, and the working of their mill was thereby delayed, and they thereby lost the profits they would otherwise have received.

On the part of the defendants, it was objected that these damages were too remote, and that the defendants were not liable with respect to them. The learned Judge left the case generally to the jury, who found a verdict with £25 damages beyond the amount paid into Court.

Whateley, in last Michaelmas Term, obtained a rule nisi for a new trial, on the ground of misdirection.

Alderson, B. We think that there ought to be a new trial in this case; but, in so doing, we deem it to be expedient and necessary to state explicitly the rule which the Judge, at the next trial, ought, in our opinion, to direct the jury to be governed by when they estimate the damages.

It is, indeed, of the last importance that we should do this; for, if the jury are left without any definite rule to guide them, it will, in such cases as these, manifestly lead to the greatest injustice. The Courts have done this on several occasions; and, in Blake v. Midland Railway Company, 18 Q.B. 93, the Court granted a new trial on this very ground, that the rule had not been definitely laid down to the jury by the learned Judge at Nisi Prius.

"There are certain established rules," this Court says, in Alder v. Keighley, 15 M. & W. 117, "according to which the jury ought to find." And the Court, in that case, adds: "and here there is a clear rule, that the amount which would have been received if the contract had been kept, is the measure of damages if the contract is broken."

Now we think the proper rule in such a case as the present is this: — Where two parties have made a contract which one of them has broken, the damages which the other party ought to receive in respect of such breach of contract should be such as may fairly and reasonably be considered either arising naturally, i.e., according to the usual course of things, from such breach of contract itself, or such as may reasonably be supposed to have been in the contemplation of both parties, at the time they made the contract, as the probable result of the breach of it. Now, if the special circumstances under which the contract was actually made were communicated by the plaintiffs to the defendants, and thus known to both parties, the damages resulting from the breach of such a contract, which they would reasonably contemplate, would be the amount of injury which would ordinarily follow from a breach of contract under these special circumstances so known and communicated. But, on the other hand, if these special circumstances were wholly unknown to the party breaking the contract, he, at the most, could only be supposed to have had in his contemplation the amount of injury which would arise generally, and in the great multitude of cases not affected by any special circumstances, from such a breach of contract. For, had the special circumstances been known, the parties might have specially provided for the breach of contract by special terms as to the damages in that case; and of this advantage it would be very unjust to deprive them. Now the above principles are those by which we think the jury ought to be guided in estimating the damages arising out of any breach of contract. It is said, that other cases such as breaches of contract in the nonpayment of money, or in the not making a good title of land, are to be treated as exceptions from this, and as governed by a conventional rule. But as, in such cases, both parties must be supposed to be cognizant of that well-known rule, these cases may, we think, be more properly classed under the rule above enunciated as to cases under known special circumstances, because there both parties may reasonably be presumed to contemplate the estimation of the amount of damages according to the conventional rule. Now, in the present case, if we are to apply the principles above laid down, we find that the only circumstances here communicated by the plaintiffs to the defendants at the time that the contract was made, were, that the article to be carried was the broken shaft of a mill, and that the plaintiffs were the millers of the mill.

But how do these circumstances shew reasonably that the profits of the mill must be stopped by an unreasonable delay in the delivery of the broken shaft by the carrier to the third person? Suppose the plaintiffs had another shaft in their possession put up or putting up at the time, and that they only wished to send back the broken shaft to the engineer who made it; it is clear that this would be quite consistent with the above circumstances, and yet the unreasonable delay in the delivery would have no effect upon the intermediate profits of the mill. Or, again, suppose that, at the time of the delivery to the carrier, the machinery of the mill had been in other respects defective, then, also, the same results would follow. Here it is true that the shaft was actually sent back to serve as a model for the new one, and that the want of a new one was the only cause of the stoppage of the mill, and that the loss of profits really arose from not sending down the new shaft in proper time, and that this arose from the delay in delivering the broken one to serve as a model. But it is obvious that, in the great multitude of cases of millers sending off broken shafts to third persons by a carrier under ordinary circumstances, such consequences would not, in all probability, have occurred; and these special circumstances were here never communicated by the plaintiffs to the defendants. It follows therefore, that the loss of profits here cannot reasonably be considered such a consequence of the breach of contract as could have been fairly and reasonably contemplated by both the parties when they made this contract. For such loss would neither have flowed naturally from the breach of this contract in the great multitude of such cases occurring under ordinary circumstances, nor were the special circumstances, which, perhaps, would have made it a reasonable and natural consequence of such breach of contract, communicated to or known by the defendants. The Judge ought, therefore, to have told the jury that upon the facts then before them they ought not to take the loss of profits into consideration at all in estimating the damages. There must therefore be a new trial in this case.

Rule absolute.